Praise for *Letters*

"Guidroz's honesty creates poignant moments; the combination of... fear, guilt, and hope makes for a potent experience..."

Kirkus Reviews

"[A] touching glimpse into the ups and downs of a father's unconditional love. Powered by raw honesty and feeling..."

BookLife/Publisher's Weekly

Guidroz's mea culpa is infused with empathy and profound introspection as he takes readers on a journey of self-discovery and redemption, reminding us that no tragedy can extinguish the flame of hope or silence the power of a father's love.

Grant Faulkner, *Executive Director, NaNoWriMo*

Riveting and refreshingly honest...this is not just another 'addict gets sober' narrative. Guidroz goes much deeper. Writing becomes his path to redemption. Eloquent and insightful, his writing moved me to tears and encouraged my soul.

Marilyn Kriete, author of *The Box Must be Empty*

Letters to My Son In Prison is a love song, with hope and reality on every single page. There is no sugar-coating here, and nothing tied up neatly with a bow, instead there are real life struggles, raw pain, and a glimpse of joy after suffering.

Becky Robinson, author of *Reach*, and CEO of Weaving Influence

I'm not a believer and I'm not a father. So why do I like Guidroz's book so much? Because *Letters to My Son in Prison* makes the grade as literature worthy of reading in depth. It's raw, straight from the heart. No treacle for effect. Ken has laid his heart and soul on the table and done it with unflinching courage.

David Booth, coauthor of *Own the Room*

Guidroz's vulnerability and downright honesty will make you cry and nod as you consider your own mistakes and lack of control over others. This story is not only inspiring, but also a testament to humanity and love.

Allison Langer, host of the popular podcast, *Writing Class Radio*

This is a must read. Although I shed a few tears, Ken's compelling message of finding hope, clinging to your spouse, and rediscovering your God is why I loved this book.

Tom Hedman, author of *A Life of Impact*

Letters to My Son in Prison is beautifully written. Guidroz writes with sensitivity and insight. His book reminds us of life's randomness, its pain and its joys.

Susan Salenger, author of *Sidelined:*
How Women Manage & Mismanage Their Health

Guidroz shares his wisdom and insight in a relatable way. This makes it easy to connect with and feel invested in the story. If you are looking for a deeply moving and inspirational read, I highly recommend this book. It will renew your faith in love and redemption and give you a sense of hope.

Barbara Legere, author of *Keven's Choice - A Mother's Journey*
Through Her Son's Mental Illness, Addiction, and Suicide

Guidroz has written an astonishing memoir. This is a powerful, agonizing, melting account of a father's love for his son. A beautifully written story told with grace and vigorous honesty.

Henry Kriete, author of *Worship the King*

Letters to My Son in Prison

How a Father and Son Found Forgiveness for an Unforgivable Crime

KEN GUIDROZ

Copyright © 2023 by Ken Guidroz

All rights reserved.
www.kenguidroz.com

No part of this publication in print or in electronic format may be reproduced, stored in a retrieval system, or transmitted in any form or by any means, electronic, mechanical, photocopying, recording, or otherwise without the prior written permission of the publisher.

The scanning, uploading, and distribution of this book without permission is a theft of the author's intellectual property. Thank you for your support of the author's rights.

Editing, design, and distribution by Bublish, Inc.

THE HOLY BIBLE, NEW INTERNATIONAL VERSION®, NIV® Copyright © 1973, 1978, 1984, 2011 by Biblica, Inc.™ Used by permission. All rights reserved worldwide.

ISBN: 978-1-647046-78-1 (paperback)
ISBN: 978-1-647046-79-8 (eBook)

COVER PHOTOGRAPH by Jen McKillop, Instagram @jenmckillopphoto_
BACK PHOTOGRAPH by Daniella Belsheim, www.danielladolencphotography.com

For Joyce, the best lunch partner in the world. And Lucas, Jess, and Chris, for showing me the heights and depths of parenthood.

"Talk to me about the truth of religion and I'll listen gladly.
Talk to me about the duty of religion and I'll listen submissively.
But don't come talking to me about the consolations of
religion or I shall suspect that you don't understand."

— C.S. Lewis, *A Grief Observed*

Contents

Author's Note

This is not just a book of letters to my son, Lucas. It's more than that. It's a story about what happened to me and him, to me and my wife, to me and my family, and to me and God. But letters did become a big part of the story. Surprisingly, they became a powerful way to communicate and connect with Lucas, and he with me. They helped me figure out what I was thinking and feeling. That is why I have included many of them in this book. They don't appear until almost halfway through the book, but when they do, either in part or the whole letter, I have edited them slightly for the retelling of our story.

While most of the names in this book are real, some have been changed to protect a person's privacy. These cases are noted in the text.

Contained within this book is a tragedy. It is the story of how a man lost his life—a man who, among other things, taught, cared for, and inspired middle school students. Because of the void his absence caused in the world, a significant portion of the proceeds of this book are being donated to a nonprofit dedicated to helping middle school students and their families. This organization finds the highest need families through the school system, and then helps them get on their feet with money and mentoring.

Finally, I have used some colorful language in this book—words I spoke or thought to myself, and words others spoke. I realize this may offend the sensibilities of some readers, and to them I sincerely apologize. But this is a book about despair and prison and the lowest moments of my life—and my son's life—experiences that tend to bring out the extremes of emotion. It was important to me to remain true to the spirit of the story.

Prologue

I did not want my son to move back home.

Lucas had hit another rough patch. He'd lost another job, gotten kicked out of his girlfriend's apartment, and was ghosting his AA sponsor. Now he needed a place to stay, so the texts to his mother started dinging like the service bell at lunchtime at Jerry's Deli. He was twenty-seven.

"Nope, I don't think we should let him move back in," I told my wife, Joyce. Then her phone dinged again.

Ha! He sure ain't gonna text me, I thought. *He remembers my little ditty: "No mon, no fun, your son. How sad, too bad, your dad."*

I knew how this move back home would unfold. He'd play the game for a few days—get up on time, help around the house, and look for a job—but soon enough his bedroom door would be closed until ten in the morning, and the knobs on his video controller would be rubbed to a shine. Then the crumbs would appear—oh, those crumbs. I'd see them on the white-tiled kitchen counter—crumbs that a normal, sober, trying-to-go-unnoticed, trying-not-to-get-kicked-out-of-your-parents'-home young man would never leave so mockingly visible.

Joyce, with her mama bear in full swing, said, "I know...it's not perfect. But what's he gonna do? Where's he gonna stay?"

I thought, *It's not our job to figure out where our twenty-seven-year-old son stays.*

Then, as if she'd read my mind, she said, "What if we lay things out super clear? Like when he has to be home and has to have a job by, and that we'll do random drug tests."

"And I become the bad cop?" I whined. "No way. I can't do that again, honey. I'm the one stuck here all day and you get to go to your job at school. I'm the one who's gonna see his slide. I'm the one who's gonna hear those ridiculous excuses. And I'm the one who's gonna have to endure those wretched crumbs on the counter."

Joyce ran her fingers over the worn grooves of our distressed-oak kitchen table.

"If we're not careful," I said softly, "he's gonna drag us down with him."

Even as I said it, though, I knew that "us" was not the real concern here. Joyce wasn't concerned about "us" and, honestly, neither was I. In thirty-plus years of marriage, we had never uttered the D-word, or even contemplated it. But this was a new level. Losing a son to opioids tested us like nothing ever had. We'd started doubting each other, snapping at each other, and misreading intentions. She'd lend him some money and I'd say, "You're enabling." I'd turn away from a need and she'd say, "You're too removed."

Without lifting her eyes from the table, she murmured, "I hear you, I really do. But we just can't—well, I can't—abandon him right now."

I whispered, "Honey, I don't think I can do this again."

She looked outside to our patio, and said, "But...where will he sleep?"

"It's not our job to figure out where he sleeps," I said meekly. "He does have wheels."

She spun toward me. "You want him sleeping in his car?"

"That's not what I said..." I pulled in my breath, not wanting to launch. What I really wanted to say was, *How did* this *become about* me *wanting him to sleep in his car?* But after a moment of chewing on my tongue, I just murmured, "What I meant was that at least he can get around."

As I thought about my car comment, though, she was actually dead-on. I *was* suggesting he could sleep in his car. But I decided to keep that little thought to myself.

Joyce stared at the table and said, "Not yet."

I waited.

"I'm not ready to cut him off," she said softly, but with conviction.

"Joyce—"

She looked up at me from the table and said, "I just couldn't live with myself if something happened to him."

That was it. That was all she needed to say. "I just couldn't live with myself," in that moment, was our version of a safe word. It stopped the conversation cold. And it's not like we had ever talked about this phrase or agreed to it as holy, but as soon as it was uttered, it was as immutable as a wedding vow. My thinking was that if Joyce couldn't live with herself because something happened to him, even if it was his own fault, after I'd forced the issue, then she *might* struggle living with me, or worse, not be *able* to live with me. And, after all we'd been through, not only with Lucas but with both our other two sons, I couldn't live with *myself* if something happened to us. I needed there to be an us. No matter the cost, no matter the pride-swallowing, no matter the concessions I might need to make, there needed to be an us.

Do other couples have a phrase like this? Do they have moments like these? I don't know. But when it happened to us, I knew it was huge. I could sense it. I felt unsteady, because after all these years of parenting, my confidence had come to an all-time low and I was mostly deferring to Joyce anyway. For the first half of my parenting life, I thought I had the gift; I thought I had the parenting gene. Handling my three boys felt as intuitive as riding a bike. But over the past fifteen years, I'd lost my mojo and felt like I was wobbling all over the road, bumping into things, and getting flat tires. My little dad gene had turned into a dad meme.

I said, "Okay, he can move back in." And when I said it, I didn't feel chastened or humiliated or put in my place. I simply accepted her words for what they were. I said, "I'll talk to him about moving back home."

Well, I did. He moved back home. And, as we expected, he slipped into old patterns—missing job interviews, sleeping in, abusing substances, forcing us to kick him out again.

About a year later, while living with his girlfriend, he was trying for the umpteenth time to get on his feet. Driving home after work one day, on a country road just outside of town, fighting off the overwhelming fatigue of a five-day heroin bender, he veered onto the thin shoulder of the road, where a man was on an afternoon bike ride. The cyclist never knew what hit him. One minute, he was navigating his front tire between the gravel shoulder and a solid white line. The next, darkness.

This is the story of what became of Lucas while he was in prison.

It's also the story of what became of me and Lucas while he was in prison, along with the unexpected role that letters played in that evolution. By the time he was incarcerated, we were out of communication options. Face-to-face was only allowed in a visiting room, talking on phones through thick glass, with what felt like the heavy cloud of ten years of disappointment hanging over us. And phone calls weren't much better. They were maxed at fifteen minutes and reverberated with inmates screaming in the background. Letters seemed to be the only option left.

This is also the story of what became of me and Joyce while he was in prison.

In the end, though, it's the story of what became of me. Not only as a dad and a husband, but also as a man whose faith was shaken by what happened. I had spent thirty years involved in a close-knit church, many of them as a leader, and I thought things would work out differently for me and my family. I thought God would bless us. So to have my family implode like it did struck at the core of my faith and made me feel like a spiritual failure, about as far away from God as I could be.

It is also the story of how I came to see my old church as part of the problem. I realized that people had become too prominent and God too small; religion had become too important and the Spirit too trivial. Instead of listening to God's voice inside of me, I cowered to the Bible-thumping strongman. I let him intimidate me. I let him guilt me. And I let him influence me to become the dad I never wanted to be.

Through this experience, I needed to find out if God was the God of the strongman. I needed to see if I could hear the Spirit's voice again. And I needed to see that God was available to imperfect fathers and imperfect families and prodigals of all kinds—whether that prodigal be a son who lost himself to opioids, or to a father who lost his way with his family and with his God.

1

Half-Inch-Thick Glass:
One Month After the Accident

L A County Jail is a notorious place. It's one of the largest jails in the world, and it's ranked as one of the ten worst in the United States.

And now it was housing my son.

I arrived on a Tuesday in June of 2016 and entered the visitor's lobby. At the check-in station, a prison guard with his hat pulled low barked at me without even looking up, "Inmate number?"

Because Joyce had checked in for our two previous visits, I had no idea what my son's inmate number was. I knew I had an appointment to see him. I knew I'd been cleared by the online prison system. And I knew not to wear gang colors or shower shoes or a low-cut blouse or short shorts. But I didn't know his inmate number.

I was tempted to lift my shoes so he could see I didn't have shower shoes on, but I thought this might not be the right time.

Peering at me from under his hat, the guard growled, "What's his name?"

"Lucas Guidroz. That's G-u-i-d-r-o-z."

The lobby had floor-to-ceiling windows on two sides and long concrete benches for visitors to sit on while waiting to go upstairs. I ambled to the area opposite the check-in booth and found a space where I could pace as I waited my turn. An older man waited patiently on a bench, along with a woman who didn't seem to notice that her three children crawled over her like a jungle gym. A young lady, maybe in her mid-twenties, also waited, wearing a tight-fitting dress and a few layers of makeup.

As I paced, my mind was all over the place, bouncing between shame and feeling out of place.

Look at what your life's become. Look where you are.

I kept my head down, putting one foot in front of the other.

I had no idea a place like this even existed.

I spun around and resumed my pacing.

I'm not like these people.

As soon as I had that thought, I corrected myself. *Stop judging them! We're all in the same boat.*

We all had a man we loved upstairs, on one of the seven floors filled with criminals. And I couldn't believe what my man had done. I wanted to see him, to talk to him, to console him, to tell him I loved him. But I also wanted to tell him how pissed off I was at him, that he deserved to be locked up in there, that he'd ruined our family, that his mom couldn't sleep at night, and that if he thought I was going to bail him out, he was freaking out of his mind.

A few minutes later, I was the only person to exit the elevator on the fourth floor. I turned to my left and walked a few steps to my assigned visiting room. Six swivel chairs were positioned in front of six booths, each partitioned by small dividers. Each booth had a phone connected to the partition, with a spiraling stainless steel cord. Separating the visitor from the inmates was a prominent feature: a yellowish, half-inch-thick glass partition.

Just like in the lobby, I couldn't sit still, so I paced while I waited for Lucas. My wife, Joyce, and I had visited him a couple times together, but this was the first time it would be just the two of us, and I was nervous. I walked to the end of the room and cupped my hands over the sides of my eyes so I could see through a mirrored glass window. Inmates came into view, milling around in light-blue prison garb, getting in line to head into what looked like a cafeteria. The men seemed so...well...old, or rough, or hardened. *My son is with these men?*

When Lucas entered the room, he smiled slightly, and his green eyes were beaming. We sat down on our stools, grabbed our phone receivers, and he said, "Hey, Pops, thanks for coming. Bet you never thought we'd be meeting *here*."

Oh, I could think of a thousand places we might have met instead: the basketball court, over sushi, at his job, or at my own kitchen table enjoying some ribs. But surely not here. My mind flashed to an eleven-year-old Lucas, peppy and rosy-faced, gabbing all the way home from summer Bible camp, telling me about his camp counselor, a basketball-playing college student at Cal State Northridge who'd made it out of South-Central LA and had turned his life around. He was now making a positive impact on the world. Lucas talked about him with such passion that I remember thinking that maybe he'd like to be that guy one day—a guy who makes a difference in the world.

My mind then flashed to eighteen-year-old Lucas, on our father–son graduation trip up to the mountains, on the heels of him leading his high school basketball team to the league championships. We'd enjoyed each other's company like we hadn't for years, talking about sports and careers and girls and marriage and futures. We were good over those three days. We were really good. More like brothers than father and son. I had the thought, as we drove away from Mammoth Mountain that Sunday, that maybe he and I would be okay, maybe the last several years of high school had just been a big hiccup.

So, as I held that phone receiver in my hand, I thought, *Nope, I never imagined meeting that boy on opposite sides of bulletproof glass at the LA County jail.*

His face was full, almost puffy—not at all what I'd expected. Then he told me about all the junk food he'd been eating and the barely-once-a-week time outdoors, and it made sense. His dark hair was meticulously gelled back in comb-width rows, and his dark-brown beard had grown full. It was closely cropped and was even neater than my beard was. He wore a crisp, yellow, short-sleeve jersey tucked into light-blue pants, cinched by a thick cotton string tied in front. Normally, inmates wore blue shirts, but while being processed into the jail system, a guard had suggested Lucas claim a mental health exemption so he could avoid being housed with the gang-riddled general population, or "gen pop," as they called it. Wisely, Lucas had agreed.

"Yeah, well, I never thought we'd be here," I said. "But hey, at least we've got this room to ourselves. Look at this." I leaned back and pointed to the other empty booths.

"I know. This never happens. I've never been the only inmate in a visiting room."

As we settled into talking through phones, I joked about the irony of him being at County, surrounded by the gang members he'd always mimicked. As a teenager, from the comfort of the suburbs, living on a street with the delightful name of Poppy Meadow, he often sang Tupac or Eminem songs about his life in the hood. His brothers would join him, and, like drunken sailors, they would rap about their "thug life." But in this visiting room, with cameras trained on us, fluorescent lights humming above us, it just wasn't that funny anymore.

I asked him how he was.

"Well, I'm doing surprisingly well," he said. "I had a slice of pizza last night."

"Okay...and...?"

"Well, it was probably the best pizza I've ever had!" His eyes rolled back. "Wait, no, no, not the best pizza—it was the best *food* I've ever had. The guards I work with shared it with us even though they're not supposed to. Man, I was in heaven."

He told me how he'd recently been given the job of porter, which included serving chow to inmates, cleaning officer areas, and distributing toilet paper throughout the facility.

Then, he steered the conversation back to me. "So, how are you? How are the brothers? And Mom? How are you all handling all this crap I've put the family through?"

I hadn't expected him to ask how *I* was doing, and I didn't really want to talk about *me*. So, I answered a couple of questions but then turned things back to him. But surprisingly, he persisted.

Look at him. Look at us. I smiled at his interest.

As we talked, though, I sensed something different in him. It wasn't necessarily a conscious thought—more a background gut feeling. Was it the unusual quietness of the visiting room? Or just us getting used to being together? I didn't really know.

Then I realized it was his eyes. They were calm. They were steady. Not darting around like I'd seen for years. He sat there and looked me steadily in the eyes. *Whoa*, I thought. *It's been a long time since I've seen him this way.*

Suddenly he stopped speaking in the middle of a sentence, and his eyes pooled with tears. His cheeks blotched red, and he dropped his head and sobbed. His shoulders heaved up and down, and he bellowed haunting, hoarse wails. He cried so loud, I expected a guard to burst into the room to see what the heck was happening. I'd never seen a man cry so hard.

As I watched him, I felt a strange separation—as if I were outside myself and wasn't even his father. I felt like a spectator. I didn't cry and felt little emotion. I think in my gut, I was glad this was happening—like nature needed to do her work.

As he calmed down, he rested his elbows on his knees, slowed his breathing, and let his head hang low. I watched without a word. Then he slowly lifted his head, looked directly at me, and said, "I am so...sorry... Dad. I'm sorry for what I've put you and the family through."

I grimaced in acknowledgment and held his gaze. Now a lump grew in my throat.

He hung his head again for several seconds. Then lifted it and said, "And, I'm..." His chin quivered, tears filled his eyes, and he winced. "I'm...I'm so sorry that I killed *Rod*."

I was stunned. He'd never said it before. This was the first time he'd voiced the victim's name.

He dropped his head again and let out a sigh. My breathing was shallow, waiting for what was next.

His eyes met mine again and he said, "And...and, I'm so sorry..." He inhaled deeply and held his breath. "...For what I did to *Valerie*."

My heart sank. This was the first time he'd named the widow.

I closed my eyes in deference to the victims.

He'd done it. He'd named them both. He'd owned the biggest mistake of his life. And, finally, *finally*, *he* was no longer the victim here. The *victims* were the victims.

He exhaled and looked down, as if the weight of his admissions had drained him.

I sat still, watching him, not wanting to ease the heaviness of the room with words. During his confession, I'd grunted my empathy, pursed my lips, or just nodded my head to show I was with him.

I don't remember how, but eventually we transitioned beyond his mea culpa into smaller talk.

As we did, in the back of my mind, I marveled at what had just happened. It was not like Lucas to break like this. Of all my sons, his was the hardest head. Jess, his older brother, was strong-willed but practical. Chris, two years younger than Lucas, learned from his two older brothers that white-flag surrender was the quickest way to happiness.

But Lucas, he fought nature. Whether it was a loosed swear word or a basketball heaved at a player on the opposing team, he was geologically slow in admission, sorrow, repentance, or humility. He treated time-outs like they were hunger strikes, embracing deprivation, ignoring hunger pains, shutting out the joyful sounds of neighborhood kids playing outside his bedroom window, narrowing his thoughts on the righteousness of his cause, stuffing his white flag even deeper in his pocket.

I remembered one time seeing him on his bed when he was eight, cross-legged, his back to the open door, looking out the window, jaw clenched, and eyes narrowed. I walked by an hour later. No flag. At hour two, still no flag. Hour three, still hunkering down with the resolve of Mahatma Gandhi. It wasn't until somewhere in that brain, deep in the cerebellum, a remote synapse fired, igniting a flicker of humility, and suddenly, without explanation, surrender appeared better than hunger—and the white flag would find its way out of his back pocket.

I was drawn back to the visiting room when a loudspeaker blared that visiting time was over.

"Let's go," shouted a guard.

I hurried into the elevator with the same six people who had visited inmates on a floor above mine. Everyone's head was down, and I wondered if they were drowning in their thoughts like I was drowning in mine. Thirty minutes before, when I'd first ridden the elevator with these people, I'd felt so different from them, like I was better than them. But now, reverberating from Lucas's breakdown, hemmed in by these elevator walls, inches from these fellow lovers-of-the-incarcerated, I felt like I was one of them. We each had someone behind glass. We each were uncertain about their future and ours. We were, after all, brothers and sisters of sadness and regret and confusion and loyalty and love for our incarcerated man.

After making my way across the street to the parking garage, I got into my car, shut the door, reached down to tilt my seat back, and let out a long sigh. *What just happened up there?* I stared into the dark garage, my mind churning like it was on high idle. *Is that what men do in jail—break like that? Was that even real?* I didn't know what to think.

After a few minutes, mental exhaustion hit me. I couldn't think anymore or try to make sense of things, so I just stared mindlessly out the windshield. As I did, I noticed that the garage ceiling seemed unusually low. In fact, for a moment, it actually seemed to be sinking toward me. The air felt heavy and humid, and I felt weighed down in my car seat, as if I was being vacuum-packed into it. It was like something or someone was telling me to stay put and absorb what had just happened. Not necessarily to make sense of it or try to understand it—just to absorb it.

I relaxed and settled into my seat. In my mind I replayed what had just happened four floors up. I saw the tears. I saw the red face. I heard the names Rod and Valerie. And I saw my son coming apart.

After a few minutes, I turned to look outside, onto the street, beyond the garage, into the brightness of the day. I squinted. From my cool, dark pocket, the hot June sun seemed so harsh, so radiant, so revealing, almost intrusive. I was not ready to go out there yet.

I don't know how long I rested there, maybe it was ten minutes, maybe thirty. But soon I knew it was time to leave. As I pressed the ignition button on my Acura, I thought, *I know what's going to happen when I leave this garage, when I drive into that sunlight, I know the world's going to be just as it's been. Lucas will still be Lucas. What he's done will still be what he's done.*

I exited onto the street, made a couple turns, and started ascending the northbound 101 on-ramp. As I merged into traffic, my premonition was correct—everything was as it had been. No matter what happened in that visiting room, no matter how many tears were shed, a man was still dead, and a widow had still been made. And I remained angry over the fact that my son was the one responsible for these tragedies.

Over the next several days, I tried to hold on to the good feelings from that visiting room. But it was useless; my pain and anger remained. In fact, my ill feelings actually increased over time. It was as if Lucas's honesty had freed me to be honest with myself. Now I could admit how pissed off I was, how abused I felt by his addiction, how mad I was about the hundred lies he'd told us, and how frustrated I was that he'd thumbed his nose at rehab.

At first, I was stunned by the acidity of my emotions. But the more I tried to neutralize them, the more they boomeranged back, sometimes with even sharper acidity. After a few days, I gave up the fight; these were not going away by sheer willpower—they needed to naturally metabolize. I just needed to feel what I felt. No matter how shocking or negative or vindictive or forbidden my emotions, I just needed to let them ride.

I journaled that week, writing myself into circles, frantic for answers, flailing for insight.

Why do I feel such vitriol toward Lucas? What do I do with these thoughts?

In a low, unguarded moment, early in the morning, seated in my office, I typed into my journal a thought that I'd woken up with. I quickly deleted it and pushed the thought away. *Nah, you don't think that.*

I relaxed at my desk, looked out the window, and enjoyed the sight of the dawn bringing definition to the mountains near me. Then the same thought interrupted my musing, so I shook my head to make it go away.

I closed my eyes, leaned back into my leather chair, and the idea appeared again. This time, however, I let it hover, I flicked it, drifted over it, looked at it from a different angle, cupped it in my hand, and then pushed it away.

But it returned. I had unearthed a truth that would not be ignored. It was a thought that felt both shameful and illuminating.

Fathers can't think this.

I pressed one key, then the next, slowly, reluctantly.

Sometimes. Some of the time, I...
wish...
I'd...
never...
had kids.
Sometimes, I hate them...for the pain and heartache they have brought me.

I stopped and stared at the words. I felt no better or worse about the secret glaring at me. The words seemed sharp and sinful, but somehow true and undeniable. Slowly, I moved my forefinger to the delete key. My sons could never see that entry.

I didn't realize it, but I would be wrestling with these feelings and rehashing these same thoughts for years. I had only just begun to uncover my own anger and frustration, and the role I had played in my son's struggles. For now, it was locked up, shrouded in fog, distorted by shame, and warped by frustration. I had no idea how to process all this, or how to connect with my son in prison, or how to be helpful to my wife, or how to help my other sons.

Lucas's words rang in my head. *I bet you never thought we'd be meeting here.*

No, son, I didn't.

2

Arraignment: One Week
After the Accident

J oyce drove us to the courthouse on the day that a superior court
judge would read every charge the State of California had against
Lucas. Those days she drove pretty much anywhere we went. Not in
the chauffeur sense, but in the therapy sense—driving was a small thing
in her life she could control. The more our world had unraveled and
become a mystery to us, the more the simple act of shifting through six
gears in her sporty two-door Scion tC hatchback soothed her nerves.

For the drive to Lucas's arraignment, however, she could have had
a hundred gears, a dozen gauges to monitor, and a thousand knobs to
turn, and it still wouldn't have been enough to relieve the pressure she
was feeling.

Since the accident a week before, Lucas had been held at a building
called Twin Towers. They were seven-story, bulky, concrete hexagon
structures in downtown LA sequestering thousands of men from society. The massive jail was a cauldron of racism and gangs and tension and
drugs. It is said that there is more gang activity and drug use in that jail
than on the streets of LA's most notorious neighborhoods.

I must admit, though, I barely thought about him over that week. I
know I should have, but the past ten years of substance abuse had worn
away my basic parental sympathies. At this point, I wasn't even going to
hire a lawyer for him. I wanted him to rely on a public defender like so
many others had to. I knew I needed to get my feelings under control,

partly because I was hoping to stay married to Joyce, but also because I knew my antipathy would level out over time.

I also knew that that first week he would be suffering from withdrawal—and that it would be done cold turkey, in a cell, with hardened men mockingly looking on. I had witnessed one weekend of withdrawal about a year earlier—the sweats, shaking, vomiting, bulging eyes, and days of fitful sleep—and had no interest in being part of that again.

Joyce had talked to him briefly a couple days before the arraignment, and he seemed to be okay—at least in one piece. Joyce said there was so much hooting, swearing, and hollering over the phone that it sounded like he was in the middle of a street brawl, and she barely got a word in. We had no idea what to expect when we saw him.

At about eight o'clock that morning, we climbed into her car for the half-hour drive to San Fernando, an old mission town in the northern part of Los Angeles. After settling into the passenger seat, I leaned over to pull my phone out of my left back pocket so I could place it in the glove compartment.

"Hey, can you google directions?" Joyce asked.

"Nah, I don't need to. I know the way."

She smirked at me and backed the car out of our driveway.

Joyce is a strong woman with a warm heart. Most people see the warm. I see the strong. She's also self-sufficient, having worked one to three jobs at a time since her preteens. She has dirty-blond hair down to her shoulders and stunning blue eyes. They're so blue that waitresses have actually stopped at our table, apologized for being so forward, and then said something like, "Those are the bluest eyes I've ever seen." And it's true. I've never seen bluer. Then—and this is my favorite part—the waitresses will comment on their sparkle.

This day, however, in that car, on that drive, heading to a courtroom, there was no sparkle in those eyes.

Joyce and I are good together. We're a good emotional match, a good spiritual match, and a good conversational match. No, actually we're a great conversational match. If I could choose only one person in the world to have lunch with, it would be Joyce. I know that's a weird metric to use when gauging a thirty-plus-year relationship, but for some reason, it just works. All the world, lunch with only one person, I'd choose Joyce.

But this day we weren't that couple. We weren't the lunch-with-one-person couple. No, we were more like the lunch-with-anyone-*but*-you couple. We just didn't handle crisis well. Instead of bringing the best out of each other, we became like cornered cats—all jumpy, bearing our claws, and doing that feline left hook thing. Joyce tended to panic and worry and fret, leaping to worst-case scenarios. I tended to underreact and pull inward and get sullen. She wanted to talk, and all I could think of was hitting the Pacific Crest Trail with our dog, Mumford, and walking and walking and walking until my legs went numb.

We hardly said a word during the thirty-minute drive, both of us swimming—well, drowning—in our thoughts. *How did this ever become us? We're driving to the courthouse—not for jury duty, not to contest a traffic ticket, not even to support a friend. No, we're driving to the courthouse to see our son in handcuffs and leg shackles, standing behind bars. We're going to hear things said about him we never thought we'd hear about any family member. This isn't our family. This isn't our son. Other families have addicts and felons and sons incarcerated at County. Not ours.*

We'd raised our family in Santa Clarita, a squeaky-clean, family-oriented suburb of LA. This was a place where you could almost eat off the streets, the lawns were clipped with the precision of a barber, and the soccer fields were full of parents with way too much interest in their kids' sports. We'd raised them going to church, not just once a week, but twice a week. Plus Sunday school.

If you'd asked us how we raised our sons before they hit the teen years, we probably would have said, "Right. We raised 'em right. We put our whole hearts into it, and we think we did okay." And when we said it, we might have had a smidge of arrogance in our voice and maybe a touch of self-righteousness. We would have been trying hard not to feel that way, but we would have.

On our drive to the courthouse, as we neared what I thought was the exit, I doubted myself. *Wait, which off-ramp is it?* I grabbed my phone from the glove box, and after the slowest upload ever in the history of Google Maps, we missed our exit. Joyce glared at the highway, her eyes narrowed, and her jaw tightened. I could feel the chill. When we finally did exit, we dropped into an old residential area with narrow streets and maybe more stop signs than I've ever seen in forty years of driving.

"You couldn't just google it." Joyce muttered. I bit my lower lip and stared out the window. My phone then piped up out of nowhere in a smug, judgy computer voice, "Make a U-turn at the next traffic signal." I lunged for my phone and silenced it with a click. Once we arrived at our final destination, it turned out not to be so final after all.

It was the wrong courthouse.

"We are the only people I know," Joyce blurted, "who are late to their own son's arraignment. And all because you knew better than Google. That's just great!"

After a few more turns, we arrived at the parking lot outside the correct courthouse. Joyce handed her credit card to the parking attendant, and he casually told us that they only accepted cash. Joyce looked at me and my stomach sank. I thought, *Well, of course they do. Why on God's green earth would they accept credit cards? It's only 2016.* I couldn't remember the last time I'd actually had cash in my pocket.

Joyce rifled through her purse and asked me to look for some cash. Without thinking, I offhandedly mused, "Why didn't you check to see if we needed cash?" As those ten words sailed over my lips, I wanted to grab them and ram them back down my throat. Of all the words to be spoken in that moment, in that car, on planet Earth, or really anywhere in the physical universe, those were the last ones that should have crossed my lips.

"Did you just say that?"

"Well, I—"

"Seriously? How is that my responsibility?"

"Um. It wasn't, uh—"

"Why didn't *you* check?!"

I stared at the dashboard.

She plunged back into her purse, fingering for bills. "You...you don't even know what's going on here. It's like...it's like you've checked out. You're just over there in la-la land."

I continued to admire the beautifully Armor All'd dashboard, repeating to myself, *Shut up, Ken. Just shut up.*

"You know, this is so like you. You expect *me* to talk to Lucas in jail; you expect *me* to get all the details on the arraignment and handle all our friends. *Then* you expect *me* to make sure we have cash for the parking lot?!"

And she was right. Since Lucas's arrest, I'd checked out; all I wanted was to be alone. I'd used work as an excuse to escape upstairs to my office when friends came over to console us. Once, I'd even slipped out in the middle of a visit to hike with Mumford. All I could think was, *I don't want consoling. I don't want pity. I don't want relating or thoughts-and-prayers or to hear about your stupid cousin who's also in jail. And I especially don't want to hear about how "God has a plan in all of this" or how "everything happens for a reason." Are you kidding me? That's what you're going to tell me right now? I can't stand the drivel. I can't take one more patronizing, mindless, nonsensical, spiritual cliché.*

A man is dead. My son did it. And now he's in jail. So just leave me alone.

Seeing we didn't have cash, the attendant pointed to a liquor store across the street that had an ATM. Joyce turned to me and said, "Go ahead, you go in. I'll get some cash."

As I started to shut the door, Joyce added, "Well, at least one of us is going to see Lucas today."

So started one of the hardest days of our lives.

A half dozen friends and my other two sons joined us at the San Fernando courthouse. The building was classic mission style, with white stucco walls, adobe roof tiles, and Saltillo paving stones lining the front walkway. After a security check, we found the courtroom where Lucas would be arraigned and were reminded that court time is very different than regular time—it's about quarter speed, I'd say. We sat in the courtroom for an hour, watching defendant after defendant appear before the judge, most of them smoldering young men, cursing at him under their breath. But there was no Lucas. I approached the bailiff and found out that he would be called much later in the day.

The rest of the morning was spent waiting in the hallway, nervously pacing, and visiting with friends. Joyce and I found it within ourselves to set aside the tension of the morning's car ride and be there for each other. As we milled about, a stout, middle-aged woman standing nearby overheard Joyce tell our friends that we did not plan on posting bail for Lucas.

The woman walked over to Joyce and asked, "You're not posting bail for your boy? Seriously? Do you know what it's like in there—the violence, the evil, the gangs? He's in danger, and if you love your son, you'll get him out of there no matter the cost."

Joyce was startled, and mumbled, "Okay..."

"If you love him," she repeated even more forcefully, "you'll get him out of there."

Joyce's eyes widened, and she nodded uncomfortably. "Okay... sounds good...uh, thank you."

I stood across the hallway, marveling at what I was witnessing.

The woman walked a few steps, but apparently wasn't convinced Joyce had gotten the message. So she spun around and called out, "I'm serious. I've seen what happens in there. Get him out." Then she stormed off.

Shell-shocked, with her mouth agape, Joyce watched her walk away. Then she turned to me, and smirked with her eyebrow arched.

I smiled, hurried over to her, and asked, "What was *that*?"

"I do *not* know."

On this one thing, Joyce and I were in complete agreement. There was no way on the planet that we would post bail for Lucas. We couldn't. Not because of money, or for his safety, or so he could detox and clear his head. Even though every parent we knew would bail their son out, we just couldn't. We were ten years into this thing, completely exhausted, and near our own breaking point. The thought of him returning to our house, with the heaviness of vehicular manslaughter hanging over his head, and his lifelong tendency to self-medicate, was utterly inconceivable. We'd move out before we let him back in. We'd move to an iceberg in Greenland before he moved back home. Heck, we'd take up residence on the calving edge of that iceberg before sharing an address with him.

There was one place for our son, only one place in the entire universe, for his own sake and everyone else's. And jail was it.

At noon, we took our gang out to lunch at a Mexican restaurant across the street from the courthouse. After all the chips and guacamole were consumed, we stood up to go back. As we did, my phone rang. I didn't recognize the number, but sensed it might be Lucas, so I cautiously slid the green circle to the right.

"Dad, hey, the lawyer here told me you're not gonna post bail? What's up?"

It was exactly what I'd expected—those exact words and that exact tone. He'd expect to be bailed out and would be pissed if he wasn't. Then he'd beg for it, plead for it, lash out for it, and even offer his soul for it. But as much as I wanted to be there for him, he'd gone too far. He'd crossed an uncrossable line. There was no rescue here.

I stammered, "Uh, yeah, I don't know about bail."

"Are you serious? You're not leaving me in here, are you?"

Normally, I'm good with words. I talk for a living. Usually, they waft over my lips without much effort. But not on this call. My tongue and brain felt frozen, like they'd been Novocained. Words dribbled out of the side of my mouth.

"Well, uh, we don't even know what the bail will be set at."

"Wait, wait, Dad, Dad, you don't know what it's like in here." His voice rose an octave. "This place is hell, you gotta get me outta here. I'm telling you, man, I'm scared for my life. This place is...I...I just gotta get outta here."

Hell? That place is hell? And you're a little scared? Are you kidding me? After what you just did, you're scared?! No, no, I'm sorry, son, you don't get to play that card. You're exactly where you need to be, and frankly you deserve it.

Well, that's what I wanted to say. But I didn't. Not one word of it. I just stuttered something pathetic.

"Listen, I'm tellin' you, I've learned my lesson. I know I've been a fuckup and haven't listened to you, but I'm telling you, I never, ever,

ever want to see this place again. I've learned, Dad, I have, I've changed. Seriously, I need your help right now. I'll pay any amount of money. I'll pay you back, I promise! I swear. I'll do anything. Just please, please, just get me outta here."

Whoa, whoa, whoa. Pay any amount of money? Seriously? Son, you've got no money. You got nothing. But hey, your dealer does. Why don't you go ask him? I'm sure he'll pony up the hundreds of dollars you just forked over to fuck yourself up over the past few weeks.

Again, that's what I wanted to say.

But I didn't. In my thirty years of parenting, in all my interactions with my sons, I had never been so bereft of words. This was my son; he needed me; of all the times he needed me, this was it. Yes, he'd screwed up and was just sobering up enough to realize the mayhem he'd caused. But still, he was my offspring. And all I could whisper was something anemic like, "I don't know, Lucas, I'll have to see what I can work out."

He went silent. He knew what that meant. "All right," he said, and hung up.

By this time, our group was walking back to the courthouse, and I was standing under a large oak tree with my phone in my hand. *Did I do the right thing? Why couldn't I find any words?*

Just then, Joyce came over and asked how the call had gone. I told her about his frame of mind, his panicked tone, and his desperate pleadings. I told her I sucked with my words and that it was *not* my finest hour as a dad.

She grabbed my hand, squeezed it, looked me in the eyes, and with a strength and conviction few other people see, she said, "Honey, there is no decision to be made here. We are *not* bailing him out."

At four thirty, after an exhausting day of pacing hallways and nursing a sour stomach, Lucas was the last inmate to appear before the judge. He was escorted to a thick chain-link metal cage with a heavily armed guard standing behind him. He faced the judge, his hands and ankles cuffed, waiting to hear the charges the State of California had against him. He wore a yellow, short-sleeve jersey and light-blue prison pants. His dark hair was ruffled, hanging into his eyes, and his face was dark and unshaven. He frowned, with a locked-jaw look, staring at the judge, and never looked over at us. We were a huddled, insecure group of loved ones longing for just a glance.

I knew Lucas was stewing over the bail discussion, but I wanted him to at least acknowledge our presence. Just a head nod or maybe a glance. Something that said, *I see you.*

The judge repositioned the swivel microphone to his mouth, cleared his throat, and read the charges:

"Gross vehicular manslaughter... While intoxicated... Hit-and-run driving... Resulting in death."

I grew heavy in my seat. The word *death* stuck in my ear like an obstruction. I lowered my eyes and forced an exhale.

As each charge was read, Lucas seemed to harden more. He clenched his jaw firmer and narrowed his eyes tighter, each word pummeling him like a gut punch.

The judge continued speaking, but all I heard were sounds bouncing around my brain.

Gross. Yes, it was gross.

Manslaughter. What a harrowing word that is. Just saying it felt like phlegm in my mouth.

Hit and run. What a coward my son had been. This was not the kind of man I thought I'd raised. But this was the kind of man he'd become—at least when he was high.

Resulting in death. A man was no longer on this earth. An innocent, unsuspecting man, riding his bike, never heard even a sound. One second, he was thinking about God knows what. The next, he met eternity. Just like that.

Joyce sat next to me, and she also slunk down in her seat. Next to her were our other two sons, Jess, thirty, and Chris, twenty-six.

Jess was strong and thickly built, with a shaved head and a full-sleeve tattoo on his left arm. Seated next to him was his Kate Middleton–esque wife of several years, Nicole. He worked as a middle school teacher, teaching students life skills, like how to relate to your parents, how to manage anxiety, and, as he put it, "how to *not* become the next school shooter." It's called Social, Emotional Learning. Ironically, the victim of the accident was also a middle school teacher. Jess didn't know him, but they had many mutual teacher friends. On the day of the accident, Jess was instructed to "immediately go home" in case any unkind words were lobbed his way for what his brother had just done.

Jess had a son of his own now, and his life had really come together over the past five years. But he, too, had been in a courtroom just like this one about ten years before. He, too, was charged with a felony, and by a mere hair—by literally seconds—he escaped that charge and the moniker of "felon" that would have followed him forever.

Chris was also muscular and stocky. He sported a military-style haircut, a holdover from the four years in the Navy he'd just finished. After high school and his half-hearted attempt at community college, his life had unraveled, and he'd succumbed to opioid abuse. He had hoped that the Navy would help him reboot and get his life back on track. But it hadn't. Once he returned home, he relapsed, and a mere month before this arraignment, he had been discharged from a rehab facility.

I looked at Chris, then at Jess, and then back up at Lucas standing inside that cage, and thought...

How did this become my family?

How did court proceedings and rehab facilities and detox programs and lawyers and the words felon, heroin, Oxy, and meth enter my family lexicon?

And how did I, a dad who really tried, who cared and prayed and went to church and prioritized family, end up with a house full of prodigals?

Just then, Lucas was escorted out of the cage, the guard grasping his arm. Before he disappeared, he looked over at us and lifted his head with a nod.

3

Special Torture

Writing—whether it was letters to Lucas in prison or to myself in my own journal—became my way of making sense of all that was happening in my life. Talking to Joyce helped, but she was in the same fog I was. A therapist proved insightful, but that only took me so far. Friends did what friends can do, until I utterly exhausted every one of them. So I was left with writing. I wrote the following in my journal some time prior to the accident.

It's a special kind of torture to watch your child slip away from you into the arms of heroin. It happens slowly, unremittingly, in fits and starts, right before your eyes. As the look in your eyes grows frantic, the look in theirs dulls. The light disappears slowly, mercilessly, until there's no fire, no spirit, no electricity. Only a muted gaze.

Because only one thing matters now.

You watch it like a slow-motion horror movie. As much as you know what's happening, as much as you want to stop it, it walks right over you as if you don't exist. You have talks, you try to inspire with a blog post, you take long drives and evening walks, you suggest a podcast or two, and you watch a documentary together. You bargain, you nudge, you raise your voice, you raise the stakes. You punish, you withhold, you yell. Then you whisper. And in your lower moments, in the moments you never dreamed you'd see, you beg, you plead. You're convinced it's just a phase, but it just keeps marching on.

Because only one thing matters now.

Then things turn and become adversarial. He crosses a line. He crosses it again. A car is dinged. Another job is lost. Stories become lavish. Tears flow easily. Excuses pile up. He says all the right words to appease you. "Yeah, yeah, no, Pops, you're right. Yeah, I'll get on that right away." But nothing changes. Ever.

Because only one thing matters now.

Things escalate. Interventions are staged. Rehabs are checked into and then escaped from in the darkness of night. Money disappears. Checks vanish. You feel like you have a thief living in your own house. You hide credit cards and jewelry. You feel exposed. Vulnerable. Unsafe. Nothing is off-limits. Friends have vanished long ago. Girlfriends are all estranged. Family means nothing.

Because only one thing matters now.

Battle lines are drawn, and you circle the wagons. You realize his enslavement could bring the two of you down. You almost turn on each other. In fact, you do. You start to blame; you point a finger; you seize on a weakness; you call her an enabler. Then you tell her she's just like her mom.

She goes quiet, she stews. How dare you. Her index finger slowly uncurls. It's you—you're the one. You're too removed, too overbearing, too harsh. You've already given up on him; he's already dead to you. And, oh yeah, you're just like your dad.

But then one day, the house goes still. Fingers curl back in. Heart rates slow. You hold your breath and listen for a sound. Silence. More silence. After a second, it hits you: she is not the problem; you are not the problem. He is the problem. It is the problem. And if we're not careful, his problem will bring us down.

Because before him, it was us. After he is long gone, it will be just us. And we need there to be an us. I need there to be an us. There must be an us!

So you scooch back-to-back, interlock elbows, cinch tightly, shuffle left, shuffle right, on the lookout for that which cares nothing about us.

4

The Accident

The accident occurred on May 25, 2016. Lucas was working as a salesperson at LA Fitness in Santa Clarita. He had worked at the club for six months and was living in town with his girlfriend of a year or so. But this day, instead of making sales pitches, bonding with potential new members, and giving tours of the facility, he was taking half-hour bathroom breaks, talking nonsensically, and slurring his words. Unbeknownst to his boss, he was high on heroin and was a week into a raging drug-and-alcohol binge. At three in the afternoon, he was told to go home and get some rest.

His ride home should have been straightforward: the 5 south, the 14 north, exit Sierra Highway, then three quick turns and he'd be in his driveway. But for some reason, he exited Highway 14 early, onto one of the narrowest, curviest roads in Santa Clarita, Placerita Canyon Road. It had two lanes and was bordered by a mere twelve-inch shoulder, which then became packed gravel. Why would he exit onto that road? Why drive the trickiest street in the valley when you're fighting off the exhaustion that comes from a weeklong bender? We would never know.

It turns out that someone else chose Placerita Canyon Road that day: a fifty-three-year-old schoolteacher named Rod Bennett. He was pedaling his bike on the slim shoulder of the road, perhaps enjoying the tall grasses swaying in the cool spring breeze, or maybe admiring the two-hundred-year-old heritage oaks that dotted the road. Whatever his reason, Rod was carefully balancing his bike tires on the narrow strip of asphalt between the white line and the packed gravel.

After a mere quarter mile, Lucas started to feel the mind swarm of fatigue, his head dropping like a medicine ball. His car veered right, and directly into the back tire of Rod's bike. The car crunched the bicycle's tire and pitched Rod backward, headfirst, into the passenger-side windshield, cartwheeling him over the car, and onto the pavement. He landed in a heap on the road and was dead before he even hit the ground.

The smash startled Lucas awake, and he pressed on his brakes to see what had happened. As he looked into his rearview mirror, he saw the crumpled body on the road and immediately knew what he'd done. Then he noticed the car behind him pull off to attend to the man. Instead of doing the same, he floored it, perhaps hoping that somehow speed could reverse time.

Lucas has no memory of what happened the rest of that day, but with the help of Jack Daniels, he slept that night. Then, as if it had all been a bad dream, he actually went to work the next day and, shockingly, made it through the workday. At quitting time, completely unplanned, he confided in a female friend that he was the one who'd killed the cyclist the day before. She immediately texted Chris the news and told him to get over to Lucas's apartment right away. Chris showed up a couple hours later.

Chris told me that when he arrived that night, Lucas was pacing his small living room, talking incessantly, waving his arms, and denying he'd been the driver. Chris pressed him for the truth three or four times, saying he'd seen the picture of a black Lexus on Facebook and it looked an awful lot like Lucas's.

"It's okay, brother," Chris said. "You can tell me what happened. Come on, man, I'm here for you."

After several hours of back-and-forth, and enough whiskey to put most men to sleep, Lucas finally broke. "Yeah, I hit him. I hit a guy on his bike yesterday and I think I killed him." He suddenly stopped pacing, looked at Chris, and said, "No, I don't *think*, I know I killed him. I know I did it." Lucas's eyes filled with tears, as if he was shocked by his own admission. Chris said he looked so different in that moment—so sad, so lost, his shoulders sagging, his head hanging low, and Chris knew their lives had changed forever.

"You gotta turn yourself in."

"I know," Lucas said. "But hey, what if I make a run to Mexico?"

"Come on, man."

Lucas took one more gulp of whiskey and asked Chris to drive him to the police station. After clearing the apartment of drugs and packing a suitcase as if he were going to a hotel, they drove to the station. Chris pulled up to the main entrance at about five in the morning, put his car in park, and said, "Brother, I'm so sorry. I'm here for you no matter what happens."

Lucas said nothing, opened the car door, and walked into the police station.

As the sun rose across the Santa Clarita valley, Chris drove east to our house on the other side of town. He was standing in our kitchen when Joyce happened to wake up at 5:30 a.m., having pieced together that Lucas was the driver of the car who'd killed the teacher.

When she saw Chris, she asked, "Luke killed that man, didn't he?"

Chris nodded and told Joyce about his night with Lucas. After a minute, she stopped him, walked to the foot of the stairs, and yelled up to me, "Ken, Ken, can you come down right away?"

I was stirred awake but didn't know what was going on.

"Hurry!" I heard her say. "Can you come downstairs right away?"

I jumped out of bed when I heard the panic and dread in her voice.

I knew that tone well—quivering, deep, raspy—unique to these kinds of situations. I'd heard it with increasing frequency over the past few years of Lucas's troubles. Now, we were just jumpy and on edge all the time. If we heard a late-night rap on the door, we'd leap off our couch, fearing another visit from the police. If Joyce called me instead of texting, I'd panic, immediately assuming the worst, and ask, "Hey there, is everything okay?" We got to the point where we refused to silence our phones, fearing that we'd get a midnight call from the ER, asking us if we were Lucas Guidroz's parents. With each dinged car, lost job, ripped shower curtain, misplaced wallet, stolen checkbook, and ruined Mother's Day, Joyce and I had only gotten more frazzled.

The first time it hit me that Lucas had a serious substance abuse problem was a couple of years after he'd graduated high school. It was a Sunday morning, and we got a call that two people very close to our family were killed the night before. Our entire family was blown away when we heard the news, and we offered our home as the place for their family members to gather that day. There were tears and wails and screams during one of the most dreadful days of my life.

Everyone was grieving in their own way, but I noticed Lucas seemed unusually out of it, almost zombie-like. He made little effort to comfort or be there for anyone in their family, even though he was very close to them. I asked him about it that night, and he just stared at me with glassy eyes, unable to articulate even a basic sentence.

Later, I pulled Chris aside to see if he could help me understand Lucas's condition. He told me that when they'd heard the news about the tragedy, Lucas immediately walked over to his chest of drawers and downed eighty milligrams of OxyContin. Chris told me it was six or seven times the amount an adult should take.

Over the next several weeks, as we all dealt with the tragedy in our own ways, I noticed that Lucas never lost his glassy eyes or his deadpan look. I also realized that I'd seen that zombie look before—I just hadn't known what it meant. Now, I knew Lucas had a real problem. This wasn't just a college thing, or a weekend thing, or a phase thing. This was a real problem.

After a few weeks of mourning, I pulled him aside again and asked him more pointedly about his abuse of substances. He stared right through me and mumbled something.

"Lucas!" I shouted. "What's up? What's going on, man?" I moved my head to catch his gaze and he didn't even notice. His eyelids fluttered at half-mast.

"Lucas. Lucas!" I clapped in his face and still got no reaction.

I wanted to grab his face and slap his cheek to wake him up. I wanted to grab his shoulders and shake him into the present. I wanted him to see me, his dad, worried to death about him, pleading with him. But none of that would have done a thing. He'd transitioned into this new world, and I was helpless to make a difference. I would witness this blank stare many times over the next eight years; it would keep me up at night; it would wake me from deep sleep; it would make me wonder if I'd ever see my son again.

His half-hearted attempt at a local community college soon came to an end. He'd heard about friends getting degrees, securing decent jobs, and settling down, but he didn't seem to care. Whistles and fake stadium cheers from the Madden video game, along with mind-altering substances, seemed to keep him just far enough from reality to not care about anything.

Soon he moved to South Pasadena to study business at Cal State LA. In a way known only to the universe, he managed to graduate. His next home was West Hollywood and he bounced from job to job, texting me an occasional "Hey Pops" every now and then, and even calling once in a while. His voice was usually obligatory, his conversations always vague, and he plowed through any personal questions by changing the subject or pretending he'd lost cell service.

He came home for a Super Bowl party one February and drank way too much. He fell asleep slouched on the sofa, his mouth wide open, and he looked like an old man. His brothers laughed and mocked him, poking him and pulling the arm he was leaning on. He didn't even wake, but just fell over and continued sleeping. They laughed. Joyce and I worried.

The next Thanksgiving, he came home to have dinner with us. He piled his plate high and stuffed his face like a starving dog. Again, his brothers teased him, telling him to eat like a human. Then he started to babble complete and utter nonsense at the table, his eyes glassy and his gaze dull. At first, we thought it was a joke, but his gibberish continued. Chris laughed. Jess called him an idiot. Joyce and I got pits in our stomachs. Then he stopped midsentence and started to nod off right at the table. After pulling his head back up, he pushed himself away from the table and clomped up the stairs. His brothers continued ribbing him, calling him names, while he zombied to the nearest bed to pass out.

Joyce and I stared at each other, bewildered. Again, we were reminded that our son was in serious trouble.

We talked him into getting therapy and counseling. He called me excitedly one day and said he'd found a female therapist he really liked. I encouraged him and offered to pay for five sessions. He seemed jazzed.

He never saw her again.

He was then kicked out of his West Hollywood apartment, his roommate having grown tired of his drug use, erratic behavior, and lost jobs. Since he had no place to go, we convinced him to detox and go to rehab. CRI-Help, an addiction and rehab facility in Los Angeles, came up as the place with the best reputation. Lucas underwent ten full days of detox and was then transferred to a residential rehab, where Joyce and I had secured him a six-month stay. It was a fabulous opportunity, complete with counseling, AA-type meetings, a place to live, and jobs he could work to get back on his feet.

He lasted all of three days. He snuck in a call to an ex-girlfriend, and within an hour she was there to pick him up.

Within a year, he was texting Joyce to see if he could stay at our house for a while.

This all happened two years before the accident. When Joyce called up to me in that raspy, quivering voice the morning she learned about the accident, I was downstairs within seconds. I hurried into the kitchen, where Joyce and Chris were talking, and she said, "Tell him."

"Lucas killed that man, the one who's been in the news. I just dropped him off at the police station."

"What?" My stomach dropped. "He killed a man?" Never did I imagine those words coming out of my mouth.

Leaning against the kitchen sink, as the sky brightened behind him, Chris said, "It was that cyclist who was killed the other day when a car hit him. That was Lucas."

I stood barefoot on the cold tile of our kitchen floor and peppered Chris with questions about the accident and the victim. I learned he was a much-loved middle school teacher in our valley, fifty-three years old, married, and had no kids. (I know I shouldn't have, but I felt massive relief over that fact.) After hearing more gruesome details about the accident, about Lucas fleeing the scene, and about his condition over the past couple days, I couldn't stand still. I left the kitchen and paced in our open living and dining room, trying to absorb what I'd heard, occasionally drawn back into the conversation between Chris and Joyce.

Eventually I went upstairs to my office so I could see what was online. I googled Rod's name and many links appeared. I clicked on newspaper sites with headlines like "Much-Loved Teacher Slain" and "Teacher on Bike Struck, Killed by Hit-and-Run Driver" and read words like "Beloved teacher was mentor and friend to so many..." and "...grief-stricken students..." My heart sank with each click. I learned that, as well as a cyclist, he was an avid outdoorsman, and loved ocean kayak fishing. He was a skilled percussionist and played marimbas in a local band. He'd recently developed an exciting new music curriculum that was all the rage at his middle school.

I landed on a picture of Rod, leaning against his bike, dressed in bike shorts and a white long-sleeve T-shirt, looking into the camera. His right hand was on his bike seat and his left was on the handlebars. His hair was clipped short, and he had a neatly trimmed goatee. He wore sunglasses and looked into the camera contentedly. He didn't seem especially happy or sad, just at peace. I stared hard at the picture, and my throat began to tighten. Tears filled my eyes as I thought, *This man is no longer here. He's gone from this earth.*

I found myself longing to see his eyes. *Why does he have sunglasses on? I need to look him in the eyes. I have something I want to say to him.* I started to well up and wanted to reach into the monitor, take off his shades, grab the sides of his face, pull him to within inches of mine, and whisper, *I'm so, so sorry my son did this to you.* But there was no grabbing of his face; there was no removing of sunglasses or begging for forgiveness; there was only the blurring of my vision as tears filled my eyes.

I leaned back in my office chair, exhausted from the avalanche of news, and an odd emotion began to stir inside of me—I had the urge to be alone. But I was already alone. But this urge was different. I needed to be somewhere dark and remote, somewhere I could let out what was stirring inside of me. I pushed back my chair and hurried down the stairs toward the garage.

When I arrived at the bottom landing, I felt like I was going to explode. I yanked open the garage door and scurried around the back of my car, looking for a place to sit. All I could find was a Home Depot bucket, which I flipped over and sat on as tears exploded from me. I curled into a ball, sinking my face into my lap, and the sheer brutality of the accident swarmed my mind: a hurtling body, a thump on the pavement, a man taken from this life. In my mind's eye, I saw a night sky with only a few, far-apart stars. They seemed to flicker at the violence.

Once the tears were spent, I stared at the floor, breathing heavily, with my elbows on my knees. Rod's wife, Valerie, came to mind. I pictured her getting the call on the afternoon of the accident, storming through her house, weeping and weeping. One day, she had a husband. The next day, none. The thought made me curl tighter. Then I imagined his young students, the confusion they must feel, the disorientation, the frustration, the anger. I curled even more into myself, trying to disappear. When I could stand it no more, I let out a silent scream that flashed brilliant white across my closed eyes. I screamed until I had no more breath.

After several minutes, I sat up and looked into a dark corner of my garage. I whispered, "I'm sorry. I'm so, so sorry." I don't really know who I whispered it to. Was it Rod? Valerie? God? The universe?

Then I tried to pray. Praying, to me, felt as instinctive as crying. But it also felt foreign now, as if I'd lost the right. What could I ask for on behalf of this man? He was dead. He was gone. I tentatively whispered, "God..." But no words followed.

Eventually I sputtered, "God, uh, please be with Rod..." I stopped and rebuked myself. *Be with him? There is no him to be with. He's gone you idiot; he's dead. And what does that even mean, to "be" with him?* I shook my head in disgust that I had patronized Rod with such a clichéd prayer.

I readied myself again, but no words came. I guess there was nothing to pray for. Or at least I had no words I could formulate. So I just bowed my head and let out a long, guttural groan—it was all the prayer I had.

Then I pictured Valerie, panicked, bewildered, pacing her house, staring at her husband's empty chair. *How she must be raging right now, how helpless she must feel, her house ringing with silence.* I looked into that same corner of the garage and asked God, *Can you be with her right now?* For some reason, "be with her" felt okay. *Please comfort her. Help her. Somehow, at this moment, comfort Valerie.*

But I had no prayers for Lucas. To be honest, I barely thought of him that day. I had nothing left in the tank for him. I had prayed for him a million times over the previous ten years, but that morning, I was dry. That morning he barely felt like a son to me. His recklessness had snuffed out the sentiments I'd had for him. I was actually relieved he was in jail. *Finally he's contained; finally he has no choice; finally he will be held accountable.* After years of near misses and losing himself to mind-numbing drugs, he had now torn a hole in the universe, and karma would extract hers.

I shed no tears for him either.

I'm also sorry to admit I wasn't available to Joyce and Chris that morning. I wish I could say I was the bigger man, the man who consoled them and comforted them on the worst day of their lives. But I can't. I just didn't have it in me.

What *did* I do that morning? Was it prayer? Or just shouting to the universe? I'm not sure. It felt a little like penance, or reckoning, or catharsis, or just plain confession.

Actually, I *do* know what I did that morning. I did the only thing I could do. In that damp garage, sitting on that five-gallon bucket, with my head buried in my lap, I told God and the universe and Rod and Valerie that I was sorry for what my son had done.

5

Fraternity of Disappointed Dads

The night after the arraignment, I stood alone in my kitchen, nursing a pomegranate vodka. The lights were dimmed, and a haunting Gregory Alan Isakov song played like a dirge over my speaker, the wailing violin pulling at my heart, and a repetitious guitar riff hypnotizing me. The judge's words rang in my ears, and the vision of Lucas's hardened face in the metal cage lingered in my mind. My throat tightened, tears filled my eyes, and I wept in the exact spot Chris had stood when he told us about the accident. When the tears stopped, my head was bowed, and the skin on my face suddenly felt heavy and loose. In that instant, I felt so old; I felt beaten-up.

The next day, everything changed. I started to feel like an outsider in my own town, like a perpetrator, or a pariah. The charges had been broadcast everywhere, and a reporter I'd watched on TV for years had shown up at my door. I declined an interview. I felt like I was no longer just me. I was the dad of that guy who killed that teacher. I was *that* father. I felt like I had a big old scarlet letter on my chest.

That afternoon, I went to LA Fitness for a workout (not the LA Fitness where Lucas had worked). When the check-in girl read my name on her computer after scanning my card, she turned quickly and stared at me. By that time, I was halfway around the circular entrance desk, and I thought, *Does she know me? Does she know I'm Lucas's father?* A flare of anger shot through me, and I glared back at her. She seemed suddenly embarrassed and quickly turned back to her monitor.

On my way to the locker room, I glanced over to the exercise machines on my right. Several heads popped up, and I could swear they were staring at me. *Do they know me? Do they know what happened?* I turned to my left to see if they might be looking at someone beyond me, but there was no one there. My body tensed and I picked up my pace to the locker room.

I went directly to a corner locker and changed into my workout clothes. My body tingled with emotional claustrophobia, and I imagined my accusers staring at me, pointing fingers and wagging their heads. In my mind, I yelled at them, *You don't know me! You don't know how hard I've tried to be a dad! I tried, dammit. I did the best I could!* I slammed my locker shut, grabbed my towel, put my head down, and made a beeline to the weight room.

The problem was, I wasn't a weight room guy. I hated lifting iron. I'd be more likely to be swinging a racket on the racquetball court or doing laps in the pool or assuming the lotus position in a darkened room. But now, that had all changed. I'd finally discovered the allure of lifting heavy objects. It made testosterone flow gloriously through the veins. It liquefied frustration and bubbled rage out of my pores. For me, weightlifting became pure therapy.

I found an open squat rack, added a few weights to the bar (trust me, very few), and then squatted as low as my imperfect knees would allow. I compressed my entire trunk into an imaginary ball, squeezing it to force the bar back up. *Ah, beautiful testosterone.* I squatted again and enjoyed the rush of adrenalin through my veins. Then, with each compression, I imagined my accusers, the girl at the front desk, the people on the exercise machines, and even some of the people in that weight room who I could swear were staring at me and judging me. In my mania, I could picture parents, whispering in their living rooms about the Guidroz family, speaking with hushed tones, and pointing their long, bony fingers at us.

After a few sets, I went to the water fountain near the racquetball courts and took a long drink. When I looked up, I saw four friends of mine exit a court and visit as you do after a game. One of them looked my way, then back to his friends, saying something to them. They all looked in my direction and I thought, *Are you talking about me?* One of them looked down and wagged his head as if he were disgusted. *Are you judging me?* Then, and I'm certain of it, one of them pointed in my direction and said something under his breath to the others, and they all snickered. A wave of heat flashed down my body and I rushed back over to my corner of the weight room.

In my delusional paranoia, I got careless. I started to heave weights around, lifting more than I should have, not paying attention to my injury-prone lower back. I thought, *Who cares anymore? What does it even matter?* I wanted to hurl my weights against the wall; I wanted to smash the mirror with my barbell; I wanted to scream at all the self-absorbed, narcissistic, egotistical weight lifters in that room; I wanted to grab my racquetball friend's face, hold it two inches from mine, and scream at him until I went hoarse, and then scream some more until his face melted in my hands; I wanted to curl into a ball in the corner of the room, disappear under the mat, and dissolve into the cement floor; I wanted to vanish, to have never been a father, or a husband, or to have ever been at all. So I pushed and jerked and heaved and cried and sweated until I could barely stand.

After I rested my final barbell, I turned around and was stunned to see that one of my friends, Jack, was standing right in front of me. He stood there for a moment, looking at me with kind eyes. Then he stepped forward and wrapped his arms around me. He squeezed much harder than I expected, so I hugged him back. Then I realized what this was: this was a father-to-father hug. It needed no words and no introduction. Men never hug like this, and Jack, in particular, was no hugger. But this was what he felt he needed to do for me. As I raged in my frustration, this was his salve. He tilted his mouth toward my ear and whispered, "If there's anything I can do, please let me know. Seriously."

Then he released me and walked away. As quickly as he'd shown up in my world, he disappeared. And there I stood, all alone, having been hugged by a fellow father. His hug didn't soothe my rage or quell my frustration or dampen my paranoia or change my life. But it was something; it was warm; it was nice; it was a beautiful thing for one man to do for another.

Jack and I weren't particularly close friends, but I realized later why he had hugged me. He, too, had raged like I had. He, too, had wondered what everyone in the community thought of him. In that very weight room, he, too, had pushed weights fueled by the adrenaline that disappointment brings. A couple of years earlier, his son had also gone off the rails and gotten into some trouble with the law, and it became public news in our town.

Had someone hugged Jack back then? I don't know. But his small act of humanity lingers with me to this day.

Jack's hug created in me a strange kinship. It was almost like we were now both part of a fraternity, a fraternity of disappointed dads—a hidden, but painfully real group of men. There were no meetings for this club, no twelve steps to follow, no sponsors to talk with. It was just a discreet fellowship of men I would never meet but would always know were there. We were broken and mystified fathers. We were fathers who didn't know what to do with the rage boiling inside of us. We were fathers who'd really tried but felt we had nothing to show for our love.

Fatherhood, for me, had never been a burden or an ill-fitting glove. I actually thought I had the dad gene. When my first son, Jess, was placed in my arms, I almost collapsed from joy. I cried a guttural cry, as if an ancient, primal part of my psyche had been woken up. In fact, I cried so hard that the people in the next room thought we had lost our baby. When two more boys followed, Lucas and Chris, I knew this role was part of my destiny. I was a dad. And I wanted to be a good dad. So I read books and attended classes and seminars; I talked to other dads and my own dad about being the best father I could be.

And I think I did a pretty good job, for about fifteen years. I did the sports thing, coaching all of them in tennis, soccer, and basketball. We did the church thing and the family vacation thing and the camping thing. I think I was tight with all three of them, maybe even closer than most dads were with their sons. When Jess was a freshman in high school, he heard about all the fights and friction most of his friends had with their dads, and he confided in me that he couldn't relate and was glad we could talk so openly.

But then something happened. It threw me off my parenting game and caused me to morph into the type of dad I never imagined I'd be. And it wasn't something insidious or evil. It was a job opportunity—an opportunity that *should* have made me a better father.

When Jess and Lucas were in middle school, I got a promotion in my pharmaceutical sales job, on the heels of receiving an MBA from Pepperdine University. Joyce was teaching at the elementary school Chris attended. At the time, life was good, family was good, and our careers were good. We lived in a great place to raise a family and were very involved in the local branch of our church. It was the kind of church where families looked out for each other, cheered for one another's kids in sports, swapped kids for sleepovers, and showed up at seven on a Saturday morning when someone needed to move. And if one of our children was called to the principal's office, we had someone with whom we could commiserate. I served as a deacon in this church, which included leading Bible studies and mentoring other couples.

The church was called the LA Church of Christ and was an offshoot of the Churches of Christ, a very popular denomination in the Southern states. (Our particular offshoot was called the International Churches of Christ.)

The church was evangelical, in that it reached out to and cared for its community. And it was Bible-believing, in that virtually every member walked into the service with a well-worn Bible under their arm. In these two ways, we loved this place.

But the church had a dark side. It was uncomfortably headstrong in its belief that not only did it have the inside scoop on what a Christian church should look like, but also in its belief that they were the *only ones* with this inside scoop. They were it. Everyone else was wrong. This doctrinal self-righteousness, narrow-mindedness, and arrogance resulted in leaders who were all those things—they led in an authoritarian and heavy-handed way. Many of the leaders suffered from a God complex, believing they were uniquely privy to God's will. Marital advice, for example, was often doled out with jarring certainty and detailed prescriptions instead of drawing couples out to help them solve their own problems. Advice on a job transfer to another city could be shockingly strong and lathered with guilt, making the member feel like career growth was unrighteous. Parenting advice was similarly narrow, with one-size-fits-all answers for almost any situation.

Joyce and I struggled with this part of the church and tried to counter it by serving as deacons with more humility and sensitivity. The fifty members from our city were just a small section of the several-thousand-member church. Because the church covered a massive region from LA to Orange County, cities like Pasadena and areas like the San Fernando Valley had mini congregations where most church life took place. Santa Clarita was up next to have its own mini congregation, and we were searching for someone to lead it.

In the fall of 1998, I was shocked when the offer to lead it came to me. I just didn't expect it. I had served in the ministry for ten years after graduating college, but that was ten years before this time, and I had no aspirations to become a pastor again. That's why I'd studied for an MBA at Pepperdine, and why Joyce had gotten a teaching credential, and why we chose jobs with decent pay, good hours, and clear boundaries—unlike our previous life in the ministry. We knew the challenges of serving full-time. We knew it was a fishbowl. And a magnifying glass. And a pressure cooker. And it could be a challenge to the teenagers of the leader—which all three of our sons would soon be. Even though I completely underestimated the pressure it would put on them, they would feel the heat of a hundred pairs of eyes on them as they went through their toughest growing-up years. My parenting decisions would be scrutinized, their behavior would be examined, and our whole family would feel like we were under a microscope.

Our marriage would also feel the pressure. Especially when things got strained between us, like if we argued on the way to church, and fifteen minutes later, I would have to stand before a hundred people and teach on grace or patience or kindness. I remembered the feeling of hypocrisy and how it could wear on my faith.

But the idea of going back into the ministry was also intriguing to us. Joyce and I could make a difference in the city we had come to love.

We could help other families. We could help married couples. I could teach the Bible in a more discreet manner, using stories and parables to motivate people to change instead of guilting them to do so. And, as naïve as this was, we thought that if our group could be a beacon of light in our congregation, we might influence our senior leadership to be humbler and more gracious.

We could do all this—and this was huge—while our sons were old enough to understand and appreciate the sacrifices we were making. They knew the jobs we'd be giving up. They'd watched us go to night school and study on weekends for degrees and credentials to better our careers. And for them to see us set it all aside for a noble purpose—that had parental inspiration written all over it.

Before I made my decision, I took eleven-year-old Lucas on a business trip to San Diego. On Amtrak, our railcar barreled down the Pacific shoreline, and we talked about this opportunity.

"Dad, you gotta do it," he said, looking up at me through his dark hair, which hung like a curtain over his green eyes. "It would be so cool, you know, you being the leader of the church."

"Well, yeah, that's funny, but you do know that it's not just about me being in charge, right?"

He looked away, embarrassed. Then he turned back to me. "Well, what do you think God wants you to do?"

I smiled and laughed inside. To him, it was *that* simple. And I wish it was. I wish I knew what God wanted. I realize that most men in my shoes would have taken a much more spiritual and elevated and providential view of my decision than I did. They would have considered it a calling, almost mystical, something they were predestined for, something they really couldn't say no to. But I didn't believe that's how God works. I didn't believe he spoke through burning bushes very often or raised people up like he did Joseph. I believed you had options in how you served God.

That night, at a sushi restaurant in La Jolla, as the sun was setting over the Pacific Ocean, with salmon belly and yellowtail tuna jiggling on our table, Lucas brought up the subject again. For an eleven-year-old, he was unusually focused on my decision, and his old soul came out in full bloom. Being over a hundred miles from home, in this very "adult" setting, with darkness settling in around us, we talked more like best friends than father and son. He even tried the sushi, which he summarily spit out. I then ordered him the conciliatory California roll. That night, Lucas asked all the right questions, made all the right observations, and as we talked, I knew exactly what I needed to do.

It was the kind of night I had dreamed of having with a son. He was now old enough to understand how tough this decision was, the job I'd be giving up, and the incredible opportunity I would be taking on. It felt like all those years of reading him Bible stories and having great talks about doing the right thing and making an impact in the world were all coming together at this restaurant.

But I don't tell of the dreaminess of this night naïvely. I tell of it nostalgically, almost painfully. I tell of it as a dad who would not experience this kind of intimacy with his son for many, many years. I tell of it as a dad who would have a hard time remembering that Lucas was ever this way.

Back at the hotel, I took a long walk on the beach by myself. With a full heart and a nervous stomach, under a full moon, I decided to accept the offer to go back into the ministry.

Things went well for the first two years, as I slid into an easy, folksy rapport with the congregation. I tried to make my sermons more inspirational than heavy, more thoughtful than preachy. Even though I was constantly prodded to be stronger and more authoritative, it just didn't suit me. I didn't want to push people in a direction they didn't want to go. I wanted them to be convinced, to be inspired, to *want* to change of their own volition. I'd seen the downside of authoritarian strong-arming, and how well it worked in the short term but how violently it could rebound later on. I hated when guilt and heavy-handedness was used on me, and I had no intention of using it on my members. So I tried to lift stories from the Bible, often about good people in some of their lower moments, to inspire those around me that they, too, could change. Jess was soon baptized in the Pacific Ocean and quickly became a leader in the teen group. Lucas and Chris enjoyed the church as well but were still too young to take an active role.

Two years in, when Jess was sixteen, he asked if we could talk. I knew something was bothering him because he hadn't seemed himself over the past couple months, missing teen functions and trying to worm his way out of more. After a Sunday service, with a box of In-N-Out burgers and steaming, salty fries on our laps, he said, "Dad, I, uh, I need to tell you something. But, you know, it's a little, um, a little hard."

I wanted to make it easy for him, so I said, "Hey, don't worry about it. You know you can tell me anything. What's on your mind?"

Pulling on his spiked blond hair, he swallowed another mouthful of fries, then said, "Well, you know, it has to do with church. It's just gotten hard, to, you know, do all that stuff at school and be a Christian..." He trailed off.

"It's okay, Jess. I can see you haven't been yourself lately, so just tell me what you're thinking. It's no problem."

As if I'd opened the spillway on a dam, he gushed all the pressure he was feeling at school. "I wanna do the right thing, but it's so hard. It feels like I'm the only person trying to live like a Christian. And it's on my mind every second of every day. And with basketball, you know, and there's this girl."

I nodded, knowing that with his recent bump up to the varsity team, he had probably gotten some added attention, especially from girls.

"Dad, it's just that no one lives like me. I mean, not one of my friends. I don't know, it's all so weird." He looked down, into his lap. "And then, you know, with your job and you being the minister, and—"

"Jess, wait, wait, wait a sec," I interrupted. "I totally get how all this stuff could weigh on you, and I get how you're feeling. But I do *not* want you worrying about my job. This is your life we're talking about, you know, your faith. And I don't want you to be concerned about what the church will think or anyone else. Seriously, this is between you and God."

His shoulders dropped, and he breathed a sigh of relief. He looked over at me, his face tinged red with acne, and he seemed, in that moment, so young and naïve, but also thoughtful and mature beyond his years.

"Thanks, Pops," he said. "Yeah, I don't know what I'm gonna do with all this. It's just gotten so messed up."

Well, maybe he wasn't willing to admit it yet, but I think he knew what he was going to do. He had found it impossible to live the Christian life at that time, and instead of being a hypocrite, and living a double life, and concocting a hundred lies to us, he believed he needed to make a clean break. And not only that, but at a mere sixteen years old, with me as the pastor of the church, he had the guts to come and talk with me about it, man-to-man. Most grown men I know wouldn't have had the guts to do that.

Jess and I talked some more, and I tried to convince him to hang in there no matter how against the current he felt, or how lonely he might be. But I could tell I made little progress. As we wrapped up our conversation in the car that day, I told him I would respect whatever decision he made.

As expected, he did disassociate himself from the church, but continued to attend and stay involved to some degree.

Little changed at home; he remained respectful, and we stayed close. He also got much closer to Lucas now that they were both outside the teen group. In fact, as time went on, their mutual disaffinity for the teen group became superglue to their relationship. They seemed to find increasing pleasure in the delicious irony that the pastor's sons were *not* involved in his own youth group. For several months this was not a problem. But then parents started to bring it up, and I knew I would eventually have to address it.

Months later, we heard through the grapevine that Jess wanted to go to the Canyon High School Winter Formal dance. Up to that point in our family, and in our rather strict church, events like that—where hormones and alcohol ran amok—were not part of our world. It sounds prudish and insular now, but as a way to buffer the influences of "the world," the church would often provide alternatives to school dances for its teen members. Jess had attended some of these functions, but now that he wasn't part of our teen group, he wanted to attend the school dance. It had been a year since our In-N-Out discussion, and I knew it was time to start making some adjustments in what we allowed him to do.

This, however, created a tricky dynamic in the church, and for me as the leader. Would I let my own kid go to a dance that other parents forbade their kids from attending? How would that play in the privacy of their homes? I could only imagine their kid saying, "Wait, what? But *Jess's dad* is letting him go, and he's *the pastor*."

I checked with my senior pastor, let's call him Bill, and in typical LA Church fashion, he strongly told me I should *not* let Jess go to the dance. "This is the time," he said, "to draw a line on what you'll accept in your family."

"Okay, fair enough, but what *reason* should I give Jess?" I asked. "You know, he has kinda taken a different path, and he's really been pushing back lately." For the first time in my life as a dad, I was starting to feel insecure about how I was handling my sons. In an almost pleading voice I said, "I just don't know how long I can keep this thing contained."

"Well, what about the other parents? Have you thought about them?" Bill asked condescendingly. "Think of how it looks with you loosening things up and compromising with your family while they try to keep it together."

"Wait, I'm not compromising here," I said. "I'm just trying to figure out how to handle sons who aren't taking the path I thought they would."

As I thought about the parents he was referring to, my stomach churned with frustration. Their teenagers seemed so different than mine—so reasonable, so willing to listen, so normal. I would sometimes watch them talk to their teens in front of me and marvel that their kid actually conversed with them—like a real human being. It made me sad because that's how it used to be with my sons. I used to be that dad who could connect with them, listen to them, and draw them out—like I had at In-N-Out that day. But not now. Over the past year, everything had changed, and it seemed to be escalating to a tipping point. I had the growing sense that Jess might be ready to throw caution to the wind.

Bill pushed me to draw a firm line with Jess. Then he played a card that was a favorite in our church to get people in line: the pride card.

"This is when you just gotta humble out, Ken. Quit being so prideful! I mean, look at the shape of your family. We both know the apple doesn't fall far from the tree."

He paused and let that last line sink in. I boiled inside as I thought about the not-so-perfect apples he had under his own tree. His son, who was two years older than Jess, was also pushing boundaries in all the same ways Jess was; he just did it quietly.

I was so exasperated by this point that I wanted to scream; I wanted to flail and yell and point fingers at his apples. But I couldn't say another word or be defensive, or I'd prove his claim that I was just being prideful and stubborn and a know-it-all. Underlying it all was the verse: "Pride goes before destruction, and a haughty spirit before a fall" from Proverbs 16:18. This verse was used as a club to get people in line. It would strike fear in the heart of any parent of a teen. He was, in essence, saying, *If you don't take my advice, you are being prideful, and you are in for a big fall with your family.*

But I wasn't being prideful; I wasn't trying to be obstinate. I was in a very tight spot, and I needed perspective and help and dialogue to help me through this quandary. But the pride challenge was like a gag—it stifled all conversation.

After talking with Bill, I still had nothing to tell Jess; I had no reason to give him for not allowing him to go to the dance. I still had a son whose hormones were flooding his veins and playing with his mind. And with each "no" I'd given him over the past several months, it only seemed to send those hormones into overdrive. The volume of our interactions had increased; he'd yell, or I'd raise my voice. Or just the opposite—he'd get sullen or lock himself in his room. We had never been so at odds, and he seemed to be growing calloused to any punishment I would give or threaten to give.

Over the next several days, before Jess asked me about the dance, I had an ominous feeling in my heart. I sensed that this was the wrong time to poke the tiger. Not right now. Not over a dance. So when Jess came up to my bedroom one afternoon and posed the question, I knew the air was charged.

"Hey, Dad, there's a dance at the school in a couple weeks, and I wanna go. Is that cool?"

"Uh, who're you thinking of going with?" I asked.

"Oh, Crystal, she wants to go with me."

"Who's Crystal?"

"Oh yeah, she's a good friend. I think you know her parents? They live over in Sand Canyon."

I walked over to my closet, pretending to fetch a shirt, trying to buy some time. "I don't think I know her or her parents. Um. I don't know, Jess."

"Dad, I know you don't know her, but she's a good person. I know that's important to you, and she is."

Jess's face started to turn pink, and my stomach churned. All I could hear in my mind was Bill's admonition: *Have a forehead of flint. Don't let his words sway you.*

"I don't know, Jess. I just don't feel comfortable with it, you know, I don't know Crystal and—"

"Comfortable with what, Dad? It's just a dance, and I really wanna go. I'm not asking you for any money or anything."

"No, no, it's not the money, I just don't know..."

"Is it because she doesn't go to our church?" Jess asked. "Dad, *I* don't go to our church. You can't keep doing this." He stared at me in disbelief.

"No, no, that's not the reason," I said, sheepishly, knowing that it was exactly the reason. "I just don't know her and—"

"Yes, it is. That's exactly why. And, Dad, that's so not right. You can't do that just cuz she doesn't go to our church."

"Jess, I'm sorry, I'm just not comfortable with it. So the answer is no."

His eyes widened. "What? Are you crazy? I can't go to the Winter Formal?" He turned around and then back toward me. "Are you, are you kidding me? I...I..."

He stormed out of the room, and I held my breath, ashamed of my blathering. Then he slammed his door and let out a long, animalistic, hoarse, haunting scream. I shivered when I heard it. It was the kind of scream that held within it anger and bitterness and exasperation.

I stood alone in my room, breathing heavily, knowing I'd blown it. I had given no good reason to Jess. I'd fostered no genuine dialogue. I'd pathetically defaulted to the age-old, extremely exasperating, conversation-ending dad line of "because I said so." And quite honestly, in that moment, I felt small; I was ashamed. Sure, I'd stood my ground and wouldn't get in trouble with my higher-ups or with the other parents. But I knew, on that afternoon, that I'd crossed a line I had never crossed before. I had poked the tiger, and now I feared he was going to roar.

I didn't know it at the time, but when Jess slammed his bedroom door, Lucas was sitting right there on his bed waiting for him. Lucas got a front-row seat to the fiery rage and Herculean exasperation that exploded in his big brother that day. He felt the heat. He witnessed the rage. And in a very real way, the recklessness that was ignited in Jess that day was also ignited in Lucas.

My two oldest sons would now bond like few brothers ever would and unite against me and Joyce. Jess ran away that night and stayed with a friend's family for a couple nights. When I saw him that Friday night at his basketball game, I told him if he ever did that again there would be no basketball. This started a cat and mouse game that would last for years. I clamped down. He started cutting himself. I drew a new line. They stopped caring that they were the pastor's sons. They were done with civility; now it was war. This nuclear fusion would radiate in our home for years.

Now, after all these years, I see that I was the one who created the perfect storm. I had utterly riled up my son when he was at his most vulnerable and emotional. The Bible doesn't say much specifically about parenting, maybe a dozen verses in all, and most of those are quite general. But it does say one thing very explicitly, specifically directed to fathers, and that is, do not exasperate or embitter your children. "Fathers, do not exasperate your children; instead, bring them up in the training and instruction of the Lord" (Ephesians 6:4). "Fathers, do not embitter your children, or they will become discouraged" (Colossians 3:21). Think of it, these are two of the most overt parental verbotens in the Bible and I had done both of them. I had painted my son into a corner and shut down discourse and provoked him and frustrated him and sucked all the oxygen out of the room. I'd pulled rank on him and created a straw man by pretending the real reason wasn't the reason. And this utterly discouraged him and frustrated him and infuriated him, because he was a live-wire, caution-to-the-wind, testosterone-fueled, end-of-his-rope, sixteen-year-old boy who saw no future in my house. It made him want to light the world on fire. And because his brother was in the room when the fuse was lit, he grabbed his brother's hand so they could light up the world together.

That night, sitting in our living room with the lights down low, Joyce and I talked about what I'd done that day. "This did not feel right," she mused, "what you, well, really, what we did with Jess today. It was just, I don't know, something was really off. I do not have a good feeling about this."

"Well, honey, maybe you don't have a good feeling because we're just not letting him get his way."

"No, that's not it," she said. "It's the *way* we did it. It just wasn't right." After a few seconds of silence, she murmured, "I don't know. I don't know what I'm feeling right now, but this was *not* a good day for our family."

I stayed silent, mulling her words, knowing that when she spoke like this, it was best to listen well.

Joyce changed that night. Until that point in our marriage, she had shared my intense desire to juggle all the competing influences in our lives: the ministry, our heavy-handed church, my pushy boss, our family, and the other families in the church. But that weekend, her mama bear stirred. As if waking up from hibernation, it stirred within her, causing her to see the world and her family in a different light. She started to curl inward, looking out for her offspring and caring less about what the members of the church thought, especially less about what the leaders in the church might pontificate on.

My mom visited us a couple months later after learning what was going on. She was a fiercely independent woman who had left her homeland of Austria to follow my Army-officer dad all over the world. His career made him a largely absentee father, and she almost single-handedly raised us four kids. Normally averse to giving unsolicited advice, when she learned what was happening with Jess and Lucas, she pulled Joyce aside. "I strongly encourage you as the mom," she counseled Joyce, "to do what *you* believe you need to do. Don't worry about what Ken thinks or what the people in the church tell you to do. Do what *you* think you should. Don't become a rebel or parade it around. Just do it quietly. God has instilled an instinct inside of you as a mom, and you need to learn to listen to it." And Joyce did just that. Even though, to her, this felt like heresy or rebellion against the church, her mama bear became the strongest urge in her life.

I wish I had changed as well. I wish I had followed Joyce's gut instinct. But I didn't. Instead, I went the other way. I doubled down on the side of my hardline church. I learned to silence my own better judgment and adopt a style of parenting that didn't suit me well at all: autocratic, heavy-handed, and unempathetic. That just wasn't me. I was much more the In-N-Out dad than this dad. But I gave in to the pressure and valued my job over parenting.

A year after the Winter Formal decision, I was delivering a sermon. Jess and Lucas were seated close to the back, slouched in their chairs, arms folded, hoodies pulled up, and they glared at me. To them, I was a hypocrite: a folksy pastor but a rigid dad. To them, I was a dad who didn't listen to them or empathize with them. And to be honest, they were right. I didn't see it at the time, but I do now. I had become an authoritarian dad, inside an authoritarian church, at war with his sons, where no one wins, and everyone loses.

Jess leaned over and whispered something to Lucas. Their shoulders shook as they chuckled. They were mocking me; I knew it. They had completely lost respect for me, and for the first time, they weren't afraid to show their disdain in public. And on that stage, I suddenly felt so small, so lost, so out of place, almost naked in front of all those people. Right there, something shifted inside of me, and what moments before had been confidence instantly turned into uncertainty. I wondered, *What am I doing up here? What do I have to say to these people when my own household is imploding? I can't do this anymore. I give up; they win.*

Suddenly I wanted to run. I felt this strange urge to disappear, to crawl off that stage, to slink over to my car, and to drive and keep driving. I had no place to go; I just had to get out of there. Now my sons knew they could get to me. Now they knew they could hurt me and undermine me. That was the day I decided to pastor no more.

Within days of this decision, however, a letter went viral among members of our worldwide family of churches. Well, it wasn't really "viral," because that wasn't a thing in 2003, but it did spread like a California wildfire, with the letter bouncing in and out of people's email. Henry Kriete, a fellow minister friend of mine from Canada, had written a letter called "Honest to God." In it, he criticized, in great detail, many of the excesses of our family of churches called the International Churches of Christ. What had started thirty years before as a group of simple Christians who wanted to live a simple Christian life, go anywhere for God, do anything, and give up everything, had become top-down leadership, guilt-based financial giving, intense accountability, and an unhealthy focus on numeric growth. Because Henry was a respected leader who had served in numerous congregations on several continents, his thirty-nine-page, well-researched, insider-rich criticism resonated completely. In churches where the excesses were rampant, it was explosive. Overnight, entire congregations, some with thousands of members, shrunk by half or more. Ministers resigned in shame, lay leaders cowered, and many members found the exit door.

But in Santa Clarita there was barely a ripple. We had long rejected those excesses and were trying to foster a much healthier church environment. But still, the leaders in our area were concerned that the fallout would affect us as well, so I was asked to stay on as the pastor until the dust settled. I agreed, but as that year progressed, the challenge of handling a church crisis and the burden of managing a struggling family became too intense. There were times I thought it would crush me. About a year after the letter came out, I resigned.

Jack's hug at LA Fitness was about twelve years after I resigned. It was then that he inducted me into the fraternity of disappointed dads. And even after all those years, I still didn't really know what had gone wrong with my family and why my sons had so rebelled against me. I didn't realize how giving in to the pressure of heavy-handed spiritual leaders, most of whom really didn't know how to handle teenagers, especially *my* teenagers, changed me and caused me to become the kind of father I didn't want to be. I didn't see how I changed from the In-N-Out dad to the Winter Formal dad, and how my sons had witnessed it and were frustrated by it and were shut down by it. I didn't see what it caused them to want to do, how they wanted to set the world on fire, and how they wanted to hurt me and hate me and get revenge on me. And I definitely didn't foresee their need to find relief through alcohol and drugs.

So, when Jack hugged me—me still feeling so lost and outcast from my community—I felt less alone, a little less the leper, a little less distant from humanity.

6

Lawyer

For several weeks after the accident, Lucas was represented by a public defender on staff at the San Fernando courthouse. She updated us on proceedings, and her expertise, warmth, and knowledge of the system was a steady hand in a troubling time.

We soon realized, however, that we needed to decide if we should hire a private attorney instead. To most parents, this was a no-brainer: *Of course you hire a private lawyer, especially if you can afford one.* Heck, to most parents, you hire one even if you can't afford it—you refinance the house or borrow from relatives or do whatever you need to do to help. But to me and Joyce, it wasn't so clear. And it wasn't a question of money. We were just so exhausted from dealing with Lucas that we thought maybe it was time for him to stand on his own.

On Saturday, after the arraignment, Jess and Chris came over to our house to discuss our dilemma. The four of us sat on our patio on a cloudy June morning, recounting how challenging the past few years had been with Lucas. Remembering Mother's Days, Thanksgivings, and two-hour phone calls which were really just talking in circles, we were leaning away from hiring a lawyer.

We talked about a disastrous intervention the family had staged around that very patio table about a year before, when Lucas had artfully turned the tables on his brothers.

Jess, as the older brother, started the meeting and told Lucas we were there to discuss his abuse problem.

Lucas snapped, "Jess, who are you, man? You've got your issues, too. Look at you, you were arrested, and now you're ratting me out like this?"

Jess leaned back, chastened.

I tried to rescue things, but then Lucas turned to Chris and said, "Are you serious, Chris? You too—you're doing this? Of all people. In fact, you're still using. Actually, I'll bet you're high right now."

Chris raised his hands but Lucas continued. "Come on, man, tell me I'm lying. Are you high right now?"

"Hey, screw you." Chris said. "I'm weaning off the stuff with Suboxone, so, yeah, I'm on Suboxone, but I'm not on heroin like you are."

"Oh, gimme a break," Lucas spat. "You guys are the last people to be ratting me out to the family. I'm outta here." And he stormed away.

I think if you could earn titles from *The Guinness Book of World Records* on such things, I'm convinced this would win for "Worst Intervention Ever."

This failed meeting was on all our minds as we discussed whether we should hire a lawyer. Jess dropped his head, shaking it back and forth.

I was puzzled. "Hey, Jess, what are you thinking?"

Without looking up, he mumbled, "But he's family. We're all he's got." He hesitated. "To be in County, that must be crazy. We used to talk about that place. He must be freaking out."

We all sat quietly, absorbing his words, putting ourselves in Lucas's shoes. After a few seconds, Joyce spoke up. "You're right." A brightness came across her face. "We gotta do it. It's the right thing to do. We need to hire someone."

In an instant, it was clear that that was the right decision. Even though a mere five seconds before, I had felt the complete opposite, once Jess and Joyce expressed themselves, all the pieces fell into place.

The next day, I worked the phone like Jerry Maguire before draft day. My job at the time was designing pension plans, many of them for law firms, so I tapped my professional network. Several lawyers gave me advice and referrals. One person led to another, and soon I had three good candidates to interview. One I talked to on the phone, and the other two I met in person. My final meeting was with an attorney named Carlo Spiga.

Joyce and I traveled to his Ventura Boulevard office early on a Sunday morning. It was his secondary office, close to home, and clearly *not* the headquarters of a white-shoe law firm. The building looked like it might be from the Tom Petty era, with the entrance on the street through an old, weathered, glass and aluminum door. Once inside, we walked up a narrow, steep staircase and entered a dimly lit office with a window overlooking Ventura Boulevard. Legal books and thick case folders were piled high on the desk and bookshelves.

Carlo was middle-aged, with a shaved head and a greying goatee. He carried himself tough, like Kojak from the 1970s TV show. But once in conversation, he proved to be warm and personable. Carlo struck me as a workman attorney, not a lawyer for the stars, and not one to chase ambulances, but one who knew the law and the system well. It became clear right away that he was an expert on LA County Jail and had personally spent a lot of time consulting with clients at Lucas's new home, Twin Towers.

As our meeting started, Carlo seemed a bit distracted, almost as if he'd met one too many parents like us—quivering, scared, and over-whelmed. He launched into a monotone spiel about what it was like at Twin Towers, the dangers of that place, how prevalent drugs were, and how the gangs operated in cooperation with the guards to keep a kind of law-of-the-jungle order. Many of his clients had told him they would prefer to be on the streets than within those walls.

As we sat across from his cluttered desk with worry written all over our faces, it felt like such a reversal of positions for me. I'd always been the person on Carlo's side of the desk. I'd been the one offering advice, con-soling bewildered parents, or trying to keep estranged couples from biting each other's heads off. But now I was the counselee. Now I was the recipient of what I hoped would be good counsel and help with our family crisis.

As he droned on about dangers and drugs and gangs, I thought, *Carlo, you're gonna start with that, seriously? No warm-up, no niceties, no comfort for us worried-to-death parents? Come on, man, you can do better than that. At least tell us you can empathize with us and that you think we seem like normal people and are probably good parents. You have a family—I can see the picture on the wall—you must know how we feel!*

He kept rambling on, tone-deaf to our body language, and I was tempted to stand up, reach across the desk, grab him by the collar, pull him to my face, and yell, *Have a heart man! Give us something to hold on to here. Okay, okay, our son blew it, and now he's in a hellhole with hundreds of hardened criminals. But come on, man, work with us!*

I was shocked at the violence of my thoughts. But I *felt* violent; I felt exposed; I felt out of control. I knew my feelings toward Carlo were pure emotion, but I couldn't contain them. Since the accident a couple weeks before, my emotions were out of control. Depression would settle in—the kind that I knew could become dangerous if I didn't handle it aggressively—and I'd just let it linger. Anger would swell, and I'd let it fly. Thoughts I would normally filter would just sail over my lips. I just didn't care anymore. My whole world had been turned upside down.

I rebuked myself for being so prickly with Carlo, a man who was just trying to help us. While pretending to take notes, all I heard was Charlie Brown's teacher's voice in my head, *Wah wah. Wah wah.*

I was sucked back into the present, however, when Carlo shifted in his seat, leaned back, and lowered his voice. "What your son really needs is hope. If you want to know my opinion, that's it. He doesn't need a high-priced lawyer or legal maneuvering. He needs hope."

Carlo paused.

"Wait, wait, what do you mean?" I asked, intrigued by the sudden silence in the room.

"Look, your son's legal situation is pretty straightforward." He rested his elbows on the desk. "I've read his file. The district attorney has a very strong case against him. They have the driver of the car behind Lucas who actually saw the accident. They have half a dozen private residence and traffic surveillance videos showing him flee the scene. They have the testimony of a coworker who saw him half an hour before the accident. The law is pretty clear about cases like this. It all adds up to between ten and sixteen years in prison."

The words "ten to sixteen" seemed to hang in the office like cigarette smoke. I quickly did the math, realizing Lucas would be almost forty by the time he got out.

"That's why he needs hope right now. *More* than legal counsel," Carlo repeated.

The word "hope" cut the smoke like a just-opened window. *My son needs hope. That's it.*

His elbows still on the desk, Carlo continued, "Look, your son's done something he never imagined he would. And now he's in a place he didn't even know existed. He's probably scared to death, and you are, too. I know it's hard; I can only imagine. You seem like good people, and he's probably a good kid, but right now, in that place, with all of this hanging over his head, he probably feels like he's in a dark tunnel and can't see his hand one inch from his face."

The room warmed.

"Your son needs to know that life will go on, that there will be another day. We don't know when, but he will have a life again." He paused, leaned back in his chair, looked at Joyce, and said, "And that's what I can give him. Because I was there one day. I was the addict. I was the man who did something he never thought he would do." His voice cracked. "I almost lost my family and everything I held dear."

He looked at me with moist eyes and said, "I'm an alcoholic. Well, I'm a recovered alcoholic. I'm a man who has been where Lucas is at. I've seen that darkness. And I made it through. I think I can help your son."

I dropped my head and tears flooded my eyes. This was it; this was our answer. This was the man to help our son.

Two months later, deep in the bowels of Twin Towers, away from the clamor of hundreds of men confined to tight quarters, in a ten-by-ten attorney-client visiting room, Lucas and Carlo spent three hours together. A mere ten minutes were spent talking about the legal part of the case. The rest of the time they talked about life and addiction and recovery and how to handle County and how to handle the darkness Lucas feared would suffocate him.

Carlo told him to be patient.

Lucas begged for help right away.

Carlo told him the darkness could remain for a long time—maybe months, maybe years—but that one day, something would happen, probably out of nowhere, and a tiny ray of light would appear, and with it, a small feeling of hope would enter his heart. He encouraged Lucas to look for it, to wait for it, to pray for it, and to believe that light would come.

Rarely in my life have I been more grateful for what another man did for my son. Carlo was a dad to Lucas when I couldn't be. I couldn't reach him; I didn't have the words, and I didn't have the hope. But Carlo did.

7

Arizona

My seesaw of emotions continued for weeks after my visit with Lucas on the fourth floor. By this time, about two months after the accident, Joyce had embraced unconditional support as her parenting ethos. To her, it was odd and disappointing that I couldn't muster the same attitude, but she gave me space and patience to come around.

For Joyce, throwing the full weight of her support behind Lucas was as natural as breathing. After her parents divorced when she was the tender age of six, they committed the ultimate divorce sin by asking her to choose which of them to live with. Completely overwhelmed by this impossible predicament, she chose neither, and spent the next six months under the care of a close family friend. After that emotional scar, she never wanted her kids to feel that kind of abandonment.

But I just couldn't get there. I needed more time.

Lucas and I had written each other a couple letters. I'd sent him some inspirational articles on Nelson Mandela and others who'd thrived in prison conditions, and he'd sent me some updates on how he was doing.

Dear Pops,

I've tried to put on a good face the last couple times I've seen you, but to be honest, I've been struggling. Sometimes, I can hardly get out of bed.

I think it's partially because I have no schedule or what we call a "program." My bunkee, on the other hand, is up at six, starting his day with exercises, then he stays busy all day. I talked to him about an hour ago and found out he's on year ten of a sixteen-year sentence. He said he lives in here like a foreigner, like he doesn't belong, like he's just passing through.

It's crazy. He's married, with two daughters about my age, and he's asked them not to make plans for when he gets out. He says he'll be okay without them. I know that sounds cruel, but he said that's what he needs to do to stay sane. He lost his dad to a heart attack a couple years ago and just had to cut off his feelings. He said he's seen men get destroyed in here trying to control their outside life from inside.

I don't know what I think about how he's handling it, but strangely, I kinda get it. You gotta protect yourself in here and prepare yourself for loss. I've had to surrender to a reality I don't control one bit, wiping out my line in the sand. I try to live in the present, not hoping for too much, setting myself up for disappointment.

Love, Lucas

I smiled at his insight and introspection. Letters like this didn't give me hope, necessarily, but they did give me hope that there might be hope one day.

As if all this with Lucas wasn't enough, I got an urgent call from my brother, Gerald, telling me that our eighty-six-year-old father was in trouble. A family friend had called to tell us our dad had just written $100,000 in checks and mailed them to someone in Jamaica. My dad believed he was paying the taxes and fees on a big sweepstakes prize he'd won. But clearly, he was being scammed. Gerald was at a business meeting and asked if I could go to Arizona to talk some sense into him.

I told Joyce the news and she grimaced. "Now? You have to go now? With all we have going on with Lucas? I can't do this on my own."

"I know, I know, the timing couldn't be worse," I said. "I just don't know what else to do."

Even though we had dealt with Lucas's incarceration completely differently—her seeking out nonjudgy friends with whom to commiserate, and me curling more and more into my own little world—we realized how much we needed each other to stay sane.

She slept on the news, and in the morning said, "You know what? You go take care of your dad, and I'll take care of Luke. That's what we'll do. Don't worry about the home front, I'll handle that. You go see what's up with your dad."

When I knocked on his door, after flying from LAX to Tucson and renting a car for the ninety-minute drive to Sierra Vista, he didn't answer. The house was dark inside, so I used my wedding band to make a loud rap on the door. I yelled out, "Pops, it's me." After no sign of life, I repositioned my car so I could shine the high beams into his living room to wake him. Still, no sign of life. I drove to a local hotel and spent the night there.

The next morning, when he answered the door, I asked what happened.

"Oh, I thought a bunch of robbers were trying to break into my house, so I grabbed my pistol out of the nightstand and was standing right here, next to the front door, ready to shoot any intruder in the thigh."

"Dad, that was me. Didn't you hear me yelling out my name?"

With no sense of irony he quipped, "Well, it's a good thing you didn't open the door."

I looked into his eyes, hoping I would see the flicker of a joke. But there was none. As I stepped toward the kitchen, I rubbed my healthy, bullet-free thigh and thought, *Now I know there is trouble in Arizona.*

Outwardly, he appeared normal, with his Paul Newman looks, wispy white hair, angular face, and sharp blue eyes. He came across confident and crisp, like the military officer he'd been for twenty-six years.

As I made my way to the kitchen, he sat on a wrought-iron barstool at the granite bar in the dining room which overlooked the kitchen. I asked him about his big win from the Publishers Clearing House Sweepstakes.

"I know, can you believe it? I won." His eyes were dancing, and his voice lilted. "I've won 2.4 million dollars and two black Mercedes-Benzes."

"So they're black?" I said with only a hint of sarcasm. "They were that specific?"

"Yep. In fact, I was just on the phone with them when you knocked. They said the transport truck was passing through Phoenix at that very moment and that they'd be here in a few hours."

"So who is 'they'?"

"Oh, it's a guy named Michael. We've been talking for weeks, and yesterday I was able to mail him the checks to pay for the taxes and delivery of my winnings."

I studied his face again, looking for any hint of awareness that he was sounding a bit crazy. He showed none.

My dad was not a naïve man. He had risen to the rank of full colonel over his military career. He'd done three tours in Vietnam, commanding a helicopter company, and had been awarded the military's third-highest honor, the Silver Star, for "conspicuous gallantry in combat." After that, he'd played cowboy on a two-thousand-acre gentleman's ranch with thirty head of cattle. Then, he'd amassed no small amount of desirable real estate in the Sierra Vista valley. He was *not* the kind of man who could be easily swindled. But here he was, completely convinced he'd won millions of dollars from a Jamaican guy named Michael.

"Dad, this isn't normal, what you're saying here. You know that, right?"

He stared at me with a dull gaze.

"This isn't how Publishers Clearing House works. They give you a check *first*, and *then* you pay the taxes out of that check. Not the other way around."

His gaze remained dull.

"No? You don't agree?"

He said nothing.

Hmmm, I thought, *what can I do?* I grabbed the check register and walked over to his side of the breakfast bar. With a soft voice, hoping not to inflame him, pointing to the entries, I said, "I see that you wrote a hundred thousand dollars in checks yesterday."

"I didn't write that much," he shot back.

"But, Dad, it's right here," I said, pointing to the entries, written almost illegibly, as if the writer might be losing his ability to write, or perhaps losing his mind.

"No way, I would never do that," he hissed as he spun away from me.

I walked back into the kitchen to regroup. Now he was pacing between the dining room and the living room, hands clasped behind his back, and his head turned away from me like a petulant child.

Watching him pace, a wave of pity came over me. I realized he didn't know what was going on. He honestly didn't. I sensed he knew something was off but couldn't quite put his finger on it. I softened my posture to make sure he didn't shut me out, and asked, "Do you mind, Dad, if we go and stop payment on those checks?"

I nervously waited for his reaction, fearing he might fly off the handle like he was prone to do. But I also had this hunch that he might find relief in my offer.

I waited. He kept professoring back and forth.

"Dad?"

Finally, he stopped and said, "Yeah, let's go do that."

I acted nonchalant, and in sixty seconds, we were in the car. While at the bank, the manager pulled me aside and confided that she was very concerned about how much cash my dad had been withdrawing. I told her that now I was involved and gave her my number.

The next day, as my dad ambled around the house aimlessly, I sensed he regretted stopping payment on those checks. I mean, life had been so much better a couple days ago, with millions of dollars in play and two new cars barreling toward his house. Now it was just boring old Ken spoiling all the fun.

He started asking me when I was going to head back home. At first, I was hurt, but then I realized he just wanted his old life back. I left a few days later, and as soon as I walked out his door, he called Michael so they could start their dance all over again.

This was my introduction to dementia. This was also my introduction to having another man in my life who needed me. Two months before, I'd been humbled as a dad. Now, I sensed I would be humbled as a son. Both of these men needed me. One was wide-eyed and terrified, shocked at the mayhem he saw around him. He needed a father, a man to be a man with him, someone to speak the truth, and someone who would comfort him. The other man was also wide-eyed and terrified. He, too, was shocked at what he saw around him—the darkness, the confusion, more darkness. He needed a son, a son to comfort him, a son to console him so that the darkness would be a little less scary. He didn't need a truth-teller. He needed a hand-holder.

When I got home from that trip, Joyce and I realized how much we had missed our nightly sanity routine. At about seven thirty, we'd wrap up our day and turn on the television, often to *Grey's Anatomy* or reruns of *Modern Family* or *Last Man Standing*. More than the shows themselves, it was the pause button on the DVR that triggered long talks about what was going on: my father's decline, Lucas's state of mind, visits to the jail, how the newspapers were reporting the proceedings, what friends were saying to us, and what we imagined everyone else in the city was saying about us.

That night, we laughed and took some liberties with an encounter we'd had with some friends a few weeks before. Our kids had all attended the same high school, and this couple had stopped by our table at Rattler's, our favorite barbecue restaurant. They seemed suspiciously eager to update us on the stellar status of their three daughters. In my typical fashion those days, not wanting to dive into a steep depression over the contrast of our families, I had no interest in hearing about their three, perfect, highly educated, newly married, getting-along-just-fine daughters. Because then they'd be obliged to ask us for an update on our far-from-perfect, barely-made-it-through-college, couldn't-hold-a-relationship-together sons.

They hinted as we visited: *Ask us about our daughters. Please, please, ask about our daughters.*

I ignored the bait and inquired, "Hey, have you had the tri tip?"

"Oh yeah, our daughter used to work here, and she loved it."

The hook flicked near my mouth, and I quickly transitioned to a question about the ribs.

"Oh, our daughter loved those, too," the mother gushed.

Just as I was going to ask about the barbecue chicken salad, the mother blurted out, "But hey, they don't have many ribs in Botswana where our daughter works for a nonprofit."

Oh crap! I'd been snagged. Now we were going to hear everything we never wanted to hear about that daughter and the other daughter and the other one.

Joyce helped set the hook by asking, "Really? Tell us more."

I slid down in my chair, the hook pulling on my lip.

"Oh, it's amazing. She's helping villagers dig wells for drinking water, so that the women don't have to travel for miles with clay pots on their heads, risking life and limb just to have enough water for their thirteen kids..."

Let me guess, I thought, *she's digging the wells by hand, clawing the earth by day, and raising funds at night.*

Knowing what I was thinking, Joyce glared at me. Then she followed up with some more questions, not just about the Botswana daughter, but about the other two as well. For several minutes, all I heard was white noise, with occasional words slipping through like "president," "magna cum laude," and "finding her place in the universe."

I gagged and went to my happy place. If they so much as reached for their phone to show us pictures, I swore I was going to call the manager.

Then there was a strange silence that yanked me back to the present. "What?" I chirped. "You want to know how our sons are doing? Oh, ha! They're doing great. Why, they're digging a few wells of their own."

Joyce's eyes pleaded, *Don't do it, don't do it.*

"A few years ago, Jess built quite a distribution business and, other than a near miss at a felony, he's doing great. Lucas, too. Why, he was just promoted to porter at County Jail, where he distributes toiletries to fellow inmates. Oh, and Chris! You must have heard he set a new world record a few years back. Yup, for the most consecutive hours of playing video games. We're so proud of them."

With stunned looks on their faces, tripping over their feet, the couple attempted an inglorious exit from the restaurant. Before they pushed the door open, I yelled, "Hey, leave us your email address and we can add you to our Christmas family newsletter list."

By this time, sitting in our living room with the DVR paused, playing back the event with no shortage of ad-lib on my part, Joyce and I were rolling in laughter. It was either laugh or cry, and we opted for the former.

8

Dexter

Communication with Lucas was frustrating. I couldn't place a call; I could only receive one. Joyce and I registered at an approved site and deposited money connected to our cell phones. This allowed Lucas to call us collect. The recording that played when I answered his call never failed to jolt me: "You have a call from an inmate at a California correctional facility..." I would think to myself, *I have a call from an inmate...at a correctional facility?*

The phones in the jail were attached to large columns in the common area of the floor. Prisoners could reserve fifteen-minute slots, and while they were talking on the phone, fellow inmates would stroll by and yell out or curse or scream. It was so consistent and excessive that I actually thought they were purposely trying to disrupt Lucas.

In-person visits weren't much better. Unlike that one soul-stirring meeting when we were alone on the fourth floor, the other visits had rooms full of people. One time, an inmate lost his cool and yelled at his wife. Another time, fellow visitors were crying and wailing.

One day, after a particularly ear-piercing phone call, I thought I'd lean into letter writing. Maybe I could say more on paper. It seemed like when we were face-to-face, the past was a leash, tethering him to the worst moment of his life and calling to mind the disappointment he'd been to me. I didn't try to make him feel that way, but it felt like the past was constantly trying to pull him—and us—under. On paper, I could speak in a more deliberate, measured tone. If I had something tough to say, I could couch it in hopeful words, making the medicine go down more easily. I could be more complimentary than I am naturally. Maybe letters could really open things up for us.

My next letter to Lucas started out tepid and mundane. I wrote about the weather and some trivial updates on the family. To keep writing about the mundane, however, felt off to me, out of touch, and, given where Lucas sat, almost disrespectful. I wanted to say something real, maybe even startling, something that would grab his attention and give him something to chew on. Nothing came to mind at first, but my mind was racing.

Then I thought about the television show *Dexter*. The title character is a mild-mannered forensic pathologist who becomes a vigilante killer, targeting people who have unfairly evaded justice, usually because of some ridiculous technicality. Dexter is driven by an inner demon he calls his "dark passenger," who has an urge to spill unrighteous blood. This dark passenger cannot be ignored, only worked around. Lucas and I had started watching the show separately and talked about it for years. The journey of this smart, charming, well-intentioned serial killer had hooked us both, season after season.

I wondered, *What if I channeled his dark passenger in some creative, connecting way?* My brain lit up. Then my fingers found the keyboard and sentences started to fly under my fingers as his story, or at least his dark passenger, found a parallel to what I wanted to say to Lucas.

Dear Lucas,

...Hey, do you remember how we always loved Dexter? *You know, his dark passenger...that uncontrollable urge inside of him to take justice into his own hands? Well, I wonder if he's a lot like us. I wonder if we each have our own dark passenger, you know, an urge we try to keep at bay, something that drives us, something we keep shoving into the back seat, hoping he'll stay where he belongs.*

Mine is anger. It's just something I've struggled to control my whole life. When it descends upon me it feels like a takeover, like I'm helpless to control it, like it's acid boring a hole in my stomach. I feel like the Hulk (without the muscles—no comment), like I'm going to explode. I have done some stupid things in a fit of rage—things that could have ended very badly in my life—but by the grace of God I've been spared.

I think you just happened to let your dark passenger grow and become a real thing. You let him out of the trunk and had him hang out with you in the back seat. You guys got comfortable with each other and when he asked to ride in the front seat, it seemed like such a harmless concession. I mean, after all, you were friends, and you were clearly the driver. So you said, "Sure."

And at first it was okay; he knew his place and you knew yours. But he's never comfortable being just the passenger. Soon he started to fiddle with the radio, turning up the volume, changing the station, turning on the A/C in winter and blasting the heat in summer.

What an asshole, you thought.

Then, in spite of all your better judgment he started to poke you in the ribs and harass you for a chance to drive. He promised it would only be for a trip around the block and then he'd hand the wheel right back to you. "Come on man," he said, "it'll help you, it'll take the edge off, and you can get some much-needed sleep."

So you did it. You let him drive. Somehow you rationalized your dark passenger taking the wheel and, at the time, it made sense to you. Hell, you could take back that steering wheel any time you wanted.

But then you realized he didn't just want to drive; he wanted control; he wanted total domination. He ordered you into the back seat where you cowered and flinched at his curses. Any time you whined, he'd smack you and put you in your place. He was in charge now; this was his car.

Then you did things you never thought you'd do. The truth became a commodity. You lied, cheated, and stole, often from those you loved the most. But no one was hurt; they hardly noticed. When the truth came to light, you flushed with embarrassment and felt dirty and cheap, like a loser. But you worked your way out of it and rationalized and cried and promised dramatic changes in your life.

But by then your dark passenger had power; he had pull. He knew your weakness; he was swimming in your bloodstream. He no longer asked to join you in the front seat, he just sat wherever the fuck he wanted.

Each round spun more and more out of control as the lies multiplied, the apologies got more dramatic, and the tears flowed heavily. Each round he got *stronger while you got weaker. Then things got dangerous. Then there were close calls and near misses. Then lives started to be touched. And ruined. The shit really hit the fan.*

I wrote like a madman, personifying Lucas's addiction with Dexter's dark passenger as creatively as I could. I think I was actually breathing heavily when I finished. I sat there, staring at my monitor, the Word document glaring back at me. What had I done? This was way too graphic to send him. But before deleting it, I thought I'd sleep on it. Maybe in the light of the next day it would be something I could send, or at least some version of it.

The next morning, after clearing my first round of emails from work, I read it from the top. Yes, it was heavy. Yes, it was strong. But it was also novel and edgy and playful in a way that I thought Lucas might enjoy and find stimulating. I thought, *What's the harm? He's got nothing but time on his hands and this will get him thinking.* After cleaning up some of the language and softening a few parts, I mailed it.

A week after I'd mailed it, I was reviewing some notes from Carlo, Lucas's lawyer. He'd warned us, "Be very careful about what you write to Lucas in jail. They screen every letter and can use them in the case against him. They look for anything potentially incriminating that the district attorney might be able to use to prosecute the case against the inmate. Any suspicious letters are sent to the DA's office for review. If they are deemed useful, the letter is placed into evidence."

Carlo had told us about a prisoner's naïve girlfriend who'd implicated him in a letter she'd written. That evidence had been used to send him to prison for ten years. Then he told us about a parent who had done the same thing. I laughed at the time, thinking, *Ha! What parent would be so stupid?*

As I stared at the note from my meeting with Carlo, my entire body flushed. Had I done that with my Dexter letter? I distinctly remembered purposely never using the words "addiction," or "heroin," or any other word that was overtly incriminating. But as I mulled it over, I began to doubt my shrewdness.

I threw my notes from Carlo aside, ran upstairs to my computer, and clicked open the Word document. I feverishly scanned the first couple of pages and saw nothing to worry about. But as I waded into my riff on Dexter and his dark passenger, my body was overcome with dread.

So you let your dark passenger drive...

...he didn't just want to drive; he wanted control...

Then you did things you never thought you'd do...Then lives started to be touched. And ruined. The shit really hit the fan.

Oh my God. I had done it. I was *that father.* I had implicated my son in a jail letter! How could I have been so naïve and stupid as to paint him as an addict who was victim to his darkest urges?

I stood up to pace the second floor of my house, my chest heaving up and down. I pulled out my phone and frantically dictated a text to Carlo. "I think I blew it. I think I wrote a bad letter to Luke. You know, the kind I shouldn't have. Please call."

Since it was the weekend, he didn't call but texted instead: "Calm down, it will probably be okay. Email the letter to me."

Like a scolded schoolboy, I sat at my desk and clicked 'send'.

The DUI part of Lucas's case was an unknown to me. Someone had witnessed him hitting the cyclist—that was not in question. Someone, and a dozen street cams, had seen him flee—that was not in question. But I knew of no hard evidence that he was high when it happened. And DUI alone would add three to six years to his sentence. Which meant that my letter, if used to prove his addiction and inebriation, could add six years to his sentence.

The thought was unbearable! I'd overdone it again. In my pathetic attempt at being whimsical and gritty and metaphorical and edgy, I had blown it.

Prove it another way, I shouted at the imaginary district attorney. *Just don't use my letter—don't make me, his own dad, the reason he spends six more years in prison.*

On Monday, Carlo emailed me and said that I'd definitely stepped over the line but that it wasn't horrible. He said that because it was metaphorical, it might be missed by the screeners at the jail and not be brought to the attention of the DA. Even if it did get flagged by the screener, he didn't think the DA would need it for evidence of a DUI, although he couldn't say for sure.

I was so mad at myself. I knew better than this. After all my years, I had learned some very hard lessons about written communications. I had committed the ALL-CAPS email sin at work and gotten reprimanded for it. I'd had to apologize after bullying a colleague with **bold words** in an emotionally charged email. I'd taken the walk of shame after sending my boss's boss a list of unsolicited suggestions. I had learned to be very careful with anything that was actually written down. And yet I had done it again; I had done it to my son, and I'd done it when he was most vulnerable.

Lucas called the next day, and I quickly asked, "Hey, did you get my letter?"

"Yeah," he said, "but, I, uh, haven't read it yet."

"Oh really? You got it but haven't read it?"

"Yeah, Dad, I'm sorry, but that was a really long letter, and to be honest, it looked kinda heavy. I'm just not sure I'm ready for that yet."

I was hurt at first, but quickly felt relief. "Oh, no, that's okay, I get it. I did kinda get carried away. Hey, why don't you just toss it, and I'll write you something else; give me another chance."

"No, I'm not saying that. I'll just read it later."

"Actually, do you mind? I'd like you to toss it so I can send you something else."

Over the next month, I was haunted by the letter. I couldn't sleep, which for me, the Roger Federer of sleep, was really saying something. My appetite shrank, which was also saying something. I daydreamed constantly. I lost more than a little time at work. I have never had something possess me so completely.

Over and over, I envisioned parts of my letter being read out loud in a courtroom. It would sound so damning, so incriminating, such a clear picture of a raging, out of control addict headed for disaster.

And sitting in that courtroom, that disaster had a name; it had a face; and it also had a widow.

I pictured the prosecutor in her dark suit, rising from her chair with a tattered copy of my letter in her hand. Before taking a step, she would look over at me and ask, "Mr. Guidroz, did you write your son a letter?"

Just the question itself would send chills through my body. *Yes, I wrote him a letter. You know I did!*

She would hold it up as she slowly walked toward me, rustling it, as if to make it more real. "This is the letter," she would say, "is it not?" *Yes.*

"Did you say Lucas had a dark passenger?"

"Did you?" *Yes.*

"Did you say that passenger drove his car?" *Well, no, that's not what I meant...*

"But it says right here, 'You let him drive. Somehow you rationalized your dark passenger taking the wheel...'" *Yeah, I wrote that, but I didn't mean it literally.*

"So you're saying Lucas had a dark passenger like Dexter did?" *Yeah, but Luke's not a murderer, I mean not like Dexter, I mean...I was just trying to...*

"Mr. Guidroz, did you tell your son that he was enslaved to that passenger?" *Yes.*

"Was that passenger drug addiction?" Silence.

"Mr. Guidroz, was that passenger abuse of substances?" *Yes.*

The courtroom would fall silent. Pure, dreadful silence. Both the prosecutor and the judge would stare at me. Joyce would look at me with pity, before dropping her head. Jess and Chris would stare in disbelief. Everyone in the courtroom would gawk at the man who had just implicated his son.

Why did I write that letter? Did I think if I wrote long enough and passionately enough that I could lead Lucas out of the darkness? Was I trying, once again, for the thousandth time, to lead him where he wasn't ready to go? Why did I always do this?

My keyboard fell silent. I swore I'd never write another word to another person for the rest of my life. I withdrew from friends and wallowed in worry. Joyce tried to console me, but I was unreachable. It brought all those years of feeling like a parental failure to a head. Why could I not, in this one all-important area, seem to do anything right? Why did I repel my sons and push them away, and just get too heavy? How could I be so uncoordinated in an area that used to be so natural to me? I felt like I was migrating into my own dad's bitterness and isolation.

Now I would just have to wait.

9

Preliminary Hearing

A month after mailing my ill-advised letter, Carlo called me to deliver the news. "The DA has officially put your letter into evidence."

I was in my living room when he called, and I just stared into space. He kept talking, but my mind drifted to all the worst-case scenarios I had envisioned.

The next big court date was the preliminary hearing. The judge would process all the evidence compiled against Lucas and determine whether a trial was warranted. For testimony, the DA would call the police who processed him when he turned himself in, the eyewitness to the accident, and a coworker who was with him a half hour before the crash. And they may possibly bring out my letter. Carlo had counseled us that a trial was unlikely, given the solidity of their case.

That morning, when we drove into the parking lot, Joyce and I were agitated. The parking attendant smiled and kindly told us where to park. As Joyce pulled into the spot and turned off the ignition, she said, "That was so nice of that man to smile like that. I needed that."

"Whew, I know," I said. "I noticed it, too. It's amazing what a smile can do."

As we walked by his booth, Joyce stepped over to him and said, "Hey, can I tell you thank you for your kindness today?"

He wrinkled his forehead.

"You smiled really nicely at us when we came in. And I know that sounds like such a small thing, but we really needed that today."

He grinned.

She stepped toward him and handed him a five-dollar bill. "Thank you," she said.

He chuckled and said, "Ha, you're welcome."

When we were about twenty feet from him, he yelled out, "Hey, thanks for noticing."

I think if Joyce could set the world right with five-dollar tips, she would.

After the security check, we rode the elevator to the third floor, which opened to a wide hallway that doubled as a reception area outside of several courtrooms. After turning left, we saw a few friends waiting for us on the far side of the hallway near our assigned courtroom. We made our way towards them.

Then I saw Valerie, the widow, with half a dozen people gathered around her, on the other side of the hallway. It was the first time I had seen her. I knew what she looked like from Facebook but hadn't seen her in person. Trying not to appear too obvious, I studied her and tried to gauge her condition. She was medium height, with shoulder-length, auburn hair, dressed casually but elegantly, and she struck me as composed and gracious. I don't know how I sensed those two qualities, but I felt them strongly. Maybe it was how she interacted with her friends, maybe it was her posture, or maybe I was just projecting.

Her family stood close to her, as if to prop her up and protect her from the harshness of this day. This would be the day when her husband's death would be talked about in excruciating detail, and she would have to relive the worst moments of her life. I wondered what she thought when she looked over at us. *Does she hate us? Does she want her pound of flesh?* I wouldn't blame her one bit if both those answers were yes.

Carlo and the DA were already inside the courtroom as we waited. The door opened, and Carlo came out to greet our group. As I reached down to get my notebook, Carlo walked over to me and Joyce and asked us to wait. He stepped back, smiled warmly, and waited for the hallway to empty. Once it was just the three of us, he leaned in, and said in a low voice, "I'm sorry, but the two of you won't be able to come into the hearing today, because you may be called as witnesses if there's a civil trial."

"Wait, what do you mean?" I asked.

"Well, because Joyce saw Lucas shortly after the accident, and because of your letter, the DA asked that both of you be excused from today's hearing in case you need to testify at his civil trial. They don't want your testimony tainted by what you hear today, and the judge agreed."

I didn't move. I couldn't move. We wouldn't be there for our son on one of the toughest days of his life. I hated that damned letter.

I quickly found a friend, named Dave, and asked him to take detailed notes of everything that was said in the courtroom. After Carlo shut the door, the hallway fell silent, and Joyce and I were alone, wrestling with our thoughts, stunned by the news we had just received.

Joyce could have so easily looked over at me and said, "You asshole. Didn't you know what you were writing? Come on, he warned us about that exact thing. It's quite simple: don't implicate your son! Why do you always do that? Why are you so direct and intense about his addiction? Couldn't you just write: *Dear Lucas, hope you're well, thinking of you, love you.*"

And she would have been right. It was my tendency to do that. She'd support him, and I'd drill down. She'd keep things light, and I'd have to keep it real until keeping it real went wrong.

But I have no idea what Joyce thought at that moment. And to be honest, I don't think I could've handled it if she'd said that. I was just too fragile; I think I would've broken down right there. But, like me, Joyce had been humbled by life and parenting. We were two chastened souls, and she was in no mood to point fingers. She knew the ricochet of blame and the circularity of grace.

As we stared into the vacant hallway, I wondered about us. *Were we one step away from breaking?* That happens to couples, you know. They lose a child to an overdose or to prison and it rips them apart. It causes them to turn on each other, and it can end a marriage.

After the hearing was over, our group convened on the sidewalk outside the courthouse so our friends could give us a blow-by-blow account of the hearing. The witnesses had made it clear, along with the testimony of the police, that Lucas was guilty of vehicular manslaughter—and that he'd been under the influence. The judge deemed that because of the overwhelming evidence, there was no need for a trial.

Our friends continued filling us in on the events, but I zoned out. *There would be no trial. There would be no reading of my letter. Those wretched pages would remain my little secret forever, never to be lifted from the dingy evidence box or be rustled in the florescent light of a courtroom or held tauntingly in front of me.*

We thanked our friends and said goodbye. Joyce and I walked to the car. Once we were seated and had pulled the doors closed, we sat in silence for a moment, both of us staring out the windshield. I inhaled a deep, long breath, closed my eyes, and exhaled slowly and deliberately. Joyce looked over at me and knew exactly what I was exhaling.

Lucas called me about an hour after getting back to jail. I expected him to be down and discouraged, but he was upbeat.

"Hey, man, you actually sound pretty good," I chirped, "considering all you've been through today."

"No, I know. That hearing was painful—just having all those people talk about me and what I did, like when I was high at work and when I hit the guy and how I fled the scene. Uh! Then it was trippy when the cops quoted exactly what I said to them when I turned myself in. I guess they tape it. Yeah, that was an out-of-body experience, almost like hearing about someone who wasn't even me. And then to have the widow sitting there, hearing everything—man, I just wanted to die."

"I know. I guess you heard we weren't allowed into the courtroom."

"Yeah, I heard. Well, maybe that's for the better. Anyway, when I got back here and walked onto my floor, this weird thing happened: I actually felt better than I had in weeks. I mean, everything looked different, and I noticed things I'd never noticed before. It was weird. I guess having all that stuff out there in the open takes some of the sting out. It's like now I've got no secrets."

"You know, now that you mention it, I can see how you'd feel that way."

We talked some more, and things ended on a good note. But then we didn't hear from him for over a week, and I started to worry. He told me later that the relief he felt that day turned dark the next. He slipped into a serious depression and could barely get out of bed for days. He dragged himself around the jail with the words from the hearing banging around his head all day long. It repeatedly sent him down the same cycle of guilt and disgust with himself for what he'd done.

10

Opa

The next legal step for Lucas was to be sentenced. Carlo predicted a ten-year sentence, with the possibility of whittling that down to half, or even less, because of Proposition 57, which was on the state ballot that fall. The proposition aimed to shrink the state's prison population by allowing inmates to reduce their sentences by completing vocational and educational programs. For nonviolent offenders—which Lucas was because his crime had been an accident—Prop 57 would allow him to reduce his sentence by two-thirds.

Between visits and phone calls, our relationship continued to improve. But I could tell he was leaning into his mom, who gave him constant encouragement and put a positive spin on everything. I tried to emulate her optimism, but I was constantly drawn back to being more realistic and circumspect. I also started to write him letters again. All my I'll-never-write-again resolutions disappeared as fast they'd appeared once I knew my Dexter letter would never see the light of the courtroom.

He also seemed to enjoy writing me. One time, he quoted from one of the books that helped him the most at County, Viktor Frankl's *Man's Search for Meaning*.

Dear Pops,

I read this great line in Frankl's book, "Suffering ceases to be suffering as soon as we form a clear and precise picture of it."

At first, I didn't really understand what he was saying, but now it's clear as day. As I look at my daily life—the boredom, the sadness, the depression, you know, everything about this life in here—I realized something kinda cool: this suffering is limited, it's finite, it's only so much and no more.

I think that's what he means when he says to form a clear and precise picture of it. The suffering is what it is, it's not going to go on forever, it's not everything. It's almost like now I'm an observer of my own life.

That may sound completely weird and stupid and confusing, but just seeing it this way helps. I just feel better. Like I can handle things now.

Love, Lucas.

This, and other letters and phone calls showed me an increasingly insightful, thoughtful Lucas—someone who was trying to make the best of a horrible situation.

Lucas and I talked several times about what was happening with my dad. In a perverse way—or maybe better put, in a roundabout way—he seemed glad that my dad's troubles took the spotlight off him. He seemed relieved to be talking about someone else whose life was spinning out of control.

Dear Lucas,

Opa's handling of the sweepstakes is only getting worse. I've been in Arizona for a month trying to keep him from giving away the farm.

After my initial visit to reverse the hundred thousand dollars' worth of checks he'd written, he struck up with those people again. Actually, he doubled down. It was like now he knew his time was limited and that I'd intervene. So he became like a rabid dog. Every day, in fact multiple times a day, he'd talk to Jamaican Michael about what he'd won, how to claim it, and where to send the tax payments so he could receive his prize.

I showed him on my laptop, using an official government website, that he was involved in a scam. But he just got misty-eyed and stared vaguely at the screen like he had no idea what was on it. Everyone in his life has talked to him about this scam—his priest, his doctor, his banker, his ranching buddies—and no one's gotten through. In fact, everyone has just become persona non grata. He declines their calls; he even declines their invitations to lunch—his favorite activity in the entire world. His house looks like a hoarder's, with stacks of letters, magazines, and receipts piled everywhere; nuts, dried fruit, and chocolate covered peanuts are placed strategically throughout the house to stave off even the hint of a hunger pang. It's spooky to see what he's become.

After some real convincing, I got him to agree to change his cell number so they couldn't reach him. It wasn't more than two days before he secretly called them from his new number.

The scammers upped their game once they knew I was around. They called more often, especially between six and three—Jamaican office hours—and ordered him to write down tracking numbers. One time, he put them on speaker phone, and I heard them demand he repeat the address of where to send cash payments. They coached him on how to lie at the UPS store so he could send envelopes of cash. He was like a dog with his ears pinned back, eager to please his abusive master. The more demanding they got, the more submissive he became. I couldn't believe this was my dad, the proud colonel, the rugged rancher.

One morning, after I heard some excited murmuring from his bedroom, he entered the kitchen with eyes ablaze and a skip in his step. I didn't know it at the time, but Michael had instructed him to get fifteen thousand dollars at the bank and mail it to a US address he'd given him. As he hurried out the door, I waited for a beat and then drove to where I thought he was going: the bank. As I walked in, he was cashing a check with a teller. I hurried over to them and blurted out that she shouldn't cash his check.

He swung his head around at me and barked, "Get the fuck out of my business!" He was a foot from my face, breathing heavily, looking like he was going to punch me. I didn't flinch and stared right back at him, even though I knew he could clock me with his right hand—you may remember, he was a national champion boxer back in his college days. I turned to the teller and told her he was getting scammed. She asked the manager to join us, but even all three of us couldn't convince him not to withdraw the money. He skedaddled out of there like OJ and was slaloming his car out of the parking lot before I could even get to mine. I thought his first stop might be the post office, so I googled it, missed a couple turns, but managed to open the front door just as the clerk was dropping his envelope into outgoing mail.

From across the room I yelled, "That envelope's got cash in it!"

The clerk spun around and tossed the envelope back to Opa, exclaiming, "You can't send cash through the mail."

In what felt like a scene from The Exorcist, Opa slowly creaked his head halfway around and delivered a string of curse words that I think are still hanging in the Arizona sky above that post office. His voice was raspy and guttural, his eyes bloodshot and bulging. He leaned toward me, and I could have sworn his shoulder twitched. But instead of punching me, he grabbed the envelope and hurried to his car.

I lost him again but guessed that he might be heading to the UPS store. I was right and it was an exact replay of the post office. This time, however, instead of The Exorcist, his reaction was On Golden Pond. He just stood in front of the clerk, his undeliverable package heavy in his hands, his shoulders sagging, and his eyes vacant. I watched from about fifteen feet away, and he seemed like such a small man, disoriented, and lost in the world. After a few seconds, he walked toward the door, passed by me without even a nod, and made his way to his car.

I walked out to see what he would do next, but his car stayed put. After a minute, I walked back and forth behind him, wondering if I should knock on his window. When another minute passed, I carefully approached the passenger side, pulled the door open just a bit, and asked if I could sit. He nodded, and I gingerly set myself down in the passenger seat, slowly shutting the door, keeping my hand on the knob in case a left hook came flying across the car.

I said nothing for a few moments and neither did he. Then I took a deep breath and asked a few questions about our wild romp around town. He responded rather casually, as if he were talking about something that had happened months before. I asked more questions, and he seemed even more distant. Then, mid-sentence, as if poked by a pang in his stomach, he chirped, "Hey, wanna grab breakfast at the Landmark Cafe?"

What? What did you just ask? I thought to myself. You wanna have breakfast with me, the person you just went all Exorcist on and almost punched?

"Dad, are you serious?" I asked, after gathering myself.

"Yeah, I'm starving," he said.

As I stared into his eyes—which seemed to be the same ones I'd looked into for fifty-eight years—I realized they didn't represent him anymore. Behind those lenses was a brain that was confused and wild with fright and unsure of anything.

My shock turned into pity, I agreed, and we went to the Landmark Cafe for the most surreal breakfast I've ever had.

You know, Lucas, that night, as I lay on my bed at my dad's house, I felt such regret. I had hoped my coming home might change things between us. This was the first time in his life when he needed me, the first time when he was the vulnerable one and I was the caregiver. And I thought the reversal of roles might reverse the coolness and shallowness that had forever characterized our relationship.

My dad was a good dad, don't get me wrong. He was kind and cordial. I've got no cigarette burns on my forearms. And he was a great provider. But I'd always hoped for more. I'd hoped for more closeness, a deeper bond—something beyond just the functionality of fatherhood and having similar DNA. I'd hoped for some intimacy, especially in our later years. Once the busyness that dominated my thirties and forties had moderated, I thought we could come to enjoy each other as two men who shared a name. Maybe travel together or get some time on the ranch. But in the car that day, when he asked if we could go to the Landmark Cafe, I realized that was not going to happen. I was too late. I had missed my chance.

And Lucas, I also realized that he and I just didn't view our relationship the same way. His generation was different than mine. To him, the words "intimacy" and "son" didn't necessarily belong in the same sentence. He was born in a more practical time, when parents were happy to have a son because he was another pair of hands to work the land. It was a time when couples would have six kids, hoping that at least four or five would survive. His own dad, my grandpa, was gruff and kick-ass and barely raised an eyebrow when my dad won a boxing scholarship to college—the first of his family to ever go. When my dad asked if he should accept the scholarship, his dad just said, "It's up to you. It's your life."

Think of it, that was my dad's model of a father. I have no doubt he saw himself as a hundred times better than his dad. Much how I see myself as a hundred times more evolved than him (well, maybe a hundred and fifty times). And, Lucas, I'm sure that when you have kids, you'll do the same.

I see it with Jess and his new son. He has such dreams and visions for that boy. He's going to do better than I did. He's going to be more nurturing, less judgmental, and more open-minded. He won't push church or religion on his son. He'll be more patient and will redirect more than discipline. And I get that. Maybe that's just how it is—we all try to do better than was done with us.

But, Lucas, it looks like you and I may have another chance. We don't have to wait for dementia to force it. I don't want you holding on to a suitcase full of regrets when I start losing my mind—whenever that may be. I don't want us to have words unsaid. Let's not do that! Let's use what's happened to you, and to us, as an excuse to say the things we want to say. Come on, man, let's break the cycle.

Love, Pops

11

Sentencing

I n our legal system, the victims (if they're alive) and the survivors get their moment to say something to the world. They're allowed to voice their anguish, frustration, and anger in the presence of the offender. Maybe not directly at him, or with the vitriol they actually feel in their hearts—although occasionally that does slip out—they get to speak their words in his presence. It's called a "Victim Impact Statement" and it's usually given on the day the inmate is sentenced for his crime. In Lucas's case, it was scheduled for a month after the preliminary hearing.

At the sentencing, Lucas would also be given a chance to say some words. Carlo had coached him on how to handle the occasion, and for days he searched for a quiet corner of the jail where he could think. He scratched out words he might say to the widow, crumpled up the paper, and started over. He filled a wastebasket with balls of paper, becoming obsessed with trying to find the right words. He had no face in his mind, only a name. (Valerie was at the preliminary hearing but he didn't know who she was in the gallery.) He told me this exercise was both excruciating and healing.

Finally, he had it. After a hundred false starts, he had the right words. He was now ready to be sentenced, to see the widow, and to say some words to her. At four in the morning on the day of his sentencing, when he was prodded off his top bunk and told to get ready for the bus ride to the courthouse, he reached into his pillowcase, pulled out the piece of paper, and stuffed it into his pocket.

Just like at the preliminary hearing, when we got to our assigned floor, both groups huddled up on opposite sides of the hallway. Then I saw several television crews and my stomach churned. Because the victim was so beloved in our community, the proceedings were all over the news, and people from the school and the cycling community had leaned on the DA's office to make sure Lucas got his just punishment.

The doors opened and we all filed in, finding our seats on opposite sides of the courtroom. The TV cameras were on the far side of the room, and Carlo sat at the defendant's table in front of us.

Lucas was escorted in with his hands cuffed behind him and his ankles shackled. He wore a yellow jersey, his hair was unkempt, and his face appeared flushed, as if he'd been crying or was extremely agitated. I found out later that the guard had just confiscated the paper on which he'd written what he wanted to say to Valerie, claiming that inmates weren't allowed to carry anything into the courtroom. Lucas pleaded with him, but he refused and gruffly seated him next to Carlo.

The judge was the same one who had presided over several appearances. He seemed to be in his early fifties, with dark hair, a trim goatee, and a kindly face. I had seen him remain patient when inmates got belligerent and mumbled curse words at him. This day, he made some introductory remarks and looked to the victims' side of the room to ask if anyone would like to make a statement. A family member spoke, as did a bandmate of the victim. They painted a picture of a warm, generous, and talented man who had recently found his place in the world. His relationships were vibrant, his professional life was expanding, and his hobbies were exciting and far-ranging. Each detail made me feel heavier in my seat. Lucas turned toward them so he could watch as they talked.

Then Valerie stood up and slowly walked to the podium. She was dressed nicely, her hair styled close to her face, and I think she had on glasses. The room fell silent when she stood, and the judge leaned back in his chair. It had been almost six months since the accident, and she was finally getting the chance to say some words. She appeared nervous and uncomfortable at the podium, fidgeting with her handkerchief. But she was also dignified and elegant and humbled and deeply sad. She held onto the podium, shifted her feet, and looked at the judge.

She talked about the man her husband was: a lover of music, a mentor to students, an avid outdoorsman. Most of all, she said, he was a lover of life, and they had come to love their life together. They had toured wine country and enjoyed nightly glasses under the stars as they recounted their day. Her voice cracked, and she looked down to gather herself. She said they had a wonderful marriage; they were good together; they had come to a very good place in their lives and could talk for hours without realizing the passage of time.

As I listened, my agony curled in on itself. It was as if she was describing my relationship with Joyce. As her voice faltered, I felt her innocence, her bewilderment, her shock that this whirlwind had slammed into her life. It reminded me of the feeling I had for her when I prayed for her in my garage six months before.

She hesitated for a moment, then said, "The house is silent without him. No more music. No more conversations. No more joy. I am in a fog without him."

I looked down and wept. Deep in my heart, I felt such darkness, such emptiness, such a void. It's exactly what I would have said if Joyce had been ripped out of my life. How victimized I would feel, how dazed, how violated.

Lucas had turned completely around to face her as she spoke. He was finally able to put a face with a name—and with the pain. He told me later that when he saw her, it all became real. It was no longer an accident that hurt a mythical man and widowed a faceless woman. No, it was a real person, with real loss, and gut-wrenching heartache. Listening to her, he started crying, his face became shiny, and mucus dripped from his nose, hanging down in long ribbons. With his hands cuffed behind him, he couldn't wipe himself with a tissue, but he seemed not to care how pathetic he looked. I wanted to reach over the banister with a tissue and wipe his face clean, but thankfully Carlo eventually noticed and awkwardly wiped his nose and face. Lucas's tears continued as long as she talked.

When Valerie was done, the judge looked at her warmly, and she returned to her seat. After she sat down, he let the silence in the room linger for several seconds. Not a paper ruffled. Not a person stirred.

Then the judge turned to Lucas and asked him if he would like to say something.

His face was still reflecting the tears when he looked toward the widow. To the best of my memory, he said, "I want you to know that I am so sorry for what I did. I—I'm just so, so sorry to you. And to your husband. I never meant for this to happen, and if I could take it back, I would in a heartbeat. And I'm sorry that I ran. I should have never left."

I ached for my son. I ached for Valerie. There were no winners here.

The judge watched Lucas with the same intensity and calmness with which he'd watched Valerie. He seemed to believe Lucas's remorse and believe that he was a good man who'd lost his way. He spoke to him like a human being, not just a felon.

When the time came for sentencing, everyone stood up, and the judge sentenced Lucas to ten years in prison. At the word "ten," Lucas dropped his head and Carlo gently placed his hand on his shoulder. Within seconds, after the judge had excused the room, the guard walked over to Lucas, reached for his arm, and escorted him out of the courtroom. Lucas looked over at us to make eye contact, but we could barely see him with the guard in the way. We waved helplessly.

I have to admit, I was proud of Lucas that day. Well, maybe not proud, it was too soon for that. A better word might be respect. I respected Lucas that day. I admired how he showed his emotions, letting tears flow while the TV cameras hummed. I loved how deeply he empathized with the widow and seemed to feel the full weight of his actions. I was so glad he looked her in the eye. And I was especially pleased that he specifically apologized for fleeing the scene.

In all, he did the one thing he could do: he told her, and the world, that he was sorry.

Yes, I respected my son that day.

12

Preacher Man

The next day, Lucas and I talked, and, just as he had after the preliminary hearing, he sounded upbeat. Other than many of the inmates giving him a hard time for crying on TV, he was relieved that another chapter of his incarceration was over—and he had survived. Now he could settle in and marshal the motivation for his prison term. He said it was like the weight on his shoulders had shifted—the burden of uncertainty now replaced by the burden of a long sentence.

But then Lucas slipped into another depression and went phone-silent for a week or so. We worried about him, and on the next call he told me that his initial post-sentencing-hope-for-a-future had boomeranged into a you-asshole-how-did-you-do-this-to-your-life present. This cycling from optimism to hopelessness had become a pattern. But each time he cycled, it seemed to drive home his mistakes, cement his brokenness, and make him a humbler man.

The next step in his incarceration was to be assigned to a prison where he would serve out the remainder of his sentence. The State of California issued these assignments at what they called a reception center. It was here that they would assess him and select the most appropriate facility for him. How far off might that be? He had no idea. County could still be his home for weeks, maybe even months.

He called one day and said, "Hey, there's a guy in here everyone calls Preacher Man. He's an older Black dude with glasses who carries his Bible around everywhere he goes and talks to everyone about God.

Anyway, he stopped me in the hallway yesterday and straight up asked me why I was in here."

I laughed and said, "Really? He asked you that?"

"Right? You're not supposed to ask people that—it's like an un-spoken rule. Anyway, he said something about me not fitting in here and wanted to know what happened to me. Then he just stood there staring at me, and I didn't know what else to do, so I told him about the accident."

"Well, whatcha gonna do?"

"Then he told me that David had killed a man, too. You know, David from the Bible. I just stared at him like I didn't know what he was talking about. Then he told me how David killed the husband of a woman he had just slept with. Yeah, when David found out she was pregnant, that's what he did. I don't remember that. At first I thought he was BSing me, but then he opened up his Bible right there and showed it to me."

"I know, I know. You don't hear that story about David very often. I mean, you normally hear about Goliath or something."

"Yeah. I couldn't believe it. But when he walked away, I must admit, I kinda felt better. I mean, not that David messed up, but yeah, I guess that's it—kinda that David messed up. I don't know, it just made me feel a little less like a loser."

Lucas was not one to talk about the Bible. Of all my three sons, he was the least naturally inclined to the spiritual. If there is a God gene, which I don't believe there is, he didn't get it (well, maybe there is). He had been raised on Bible stories from his earliest days and had always asked great questions and recalled the stories with surprising accuracy. He just never seemed to make a personal connection with God or the Bible.

The closest he came to personal faith was in his summer between sixth and seventh grade. He went to Bible camp in the mountains, as he had for years, but upon his return, I could tell he was different—he was more subdued. I remember when he crawled into the car, he looked over at me, his dark hair long and framing his face, his eyes bright, his jaw squared, and he seemed to be an eleven-year-old boy who was trying to be serious with his dad. I could tell he wanted to talk so I asked if he'd like to grab lunch at the Bear Pit before heading home.

The Bear Pit was our favorite barbeque joint in the Valley and the place of many family memories. It was a relic from the 1970s, with paisley light shades, pine wood paneling, Kodachrome pictures on the wall, and linoleum countertops. The waitresses were all gruff, no-nonsense women between forty and sixty years old, some of whom had been there since the restaurant had opened. The menu had hardly changed over the years, and the style of slow roasting meat for nine to ten hours, over California red oak, was done exactly as the first pitmaster had done it almost fifty years before. It gave meat an earthy, caramelized, smoky flavor that seemed to ignite a spark in the oldest, most primitive part of the brain, the olfactory bulb. The thought of going to the Bear Pit after eating camp food for a week lit up Lucas's face like one of those paisley light shades.

It was at this restaurant, for that hour, that I saw the one and only spark of spirituality rise up in Lucas over his lifetime. He talked in great detail about how his cabin counselor came to know God after being raised in an abusive home where there were drugs and fighting. This counselor found his only refuge on the basketball court, sometimes spending all day there and most of the night, playing and dribbling and hanging out. Lucas was drawn to his honesty when he shared about the haunting loneliness he felt, and how he'd cry himself to sleep many nights. Then this counselor shared about how he had come to know God while a student at Cal State Northridge, and now he had a new purpose in life and wanted to make a difference in the world.

Lucas told me about "group," when the eight boys in his cabin would sit in a circle at the end of the day and talk about what had touched them from the sharing. He used the words "God" and "courage" and "forgiveness" like he never had.

I wondered, *Is this it? Is this when he's going to turn to God?* But, unfortunately, the afterglow from camp lasted only a few weeks. As it always had, the roaring current of the world pulled him back in—the influence of friends, music, and media.

That had been sixteen years ago. Now we were on the phone talking about David, of all people. Now Lucas was finding solace in David's weakness. Now he was contending with a persuasive guy named Preacher Man, telling him that *he* had something in common with David.

After the call, I went up to my office, leaned back in my brown leather chair, placed my legs on the desk, and stared out my window, thinking about David and Bathsheba. The story was intriguing, to be sure, with plot twists and elements of lust, sex, deceit, scheming, and murder. But it wasn't just salacious. It was more than that. It had interesting characters, punch-in-the-face confrontation, the crafty use of parable, and an epic poem at the end about brokenness. This poem was unlike anything else in all of literature. If you factor in the man, his character, the throne, how much he had to lose, the creativity of Nathan's confrontation, and the sincerity of David's remorse, what's known today as Psalm 51 is an unmatched, elegant, poetic description of a man in a broken state.

It had been years since I'd read the story, so I reached for my brown leather Bible from the bookshelf, and it had a layer of dust on it. *Had it been that long?* In my former life, I used to rail against people who let their Bible gather dust. Now I was that guy.

I sprayed a paper towel with water, wiped off the dust, took a deep breath, and opened it to David and Bathsheba. The translucent, onion-skin pages felt comfortable in my fingers, the supple brown leather lay flat and heavy on my walnut desk, and I was brought back to what I used to do all the time. But this time, the story read differently. It was like I was reading it for the first time, not through the lens of religion or doctrine or for the purpose of teaching it, but reading it for what it was, for what actually happened. I envisioned it. I played it out in my mind. I could see her bathing and him peering and all the other elements of the story. It was so freeing to read the Bible that way.

Then I got a brainstorm: I'd write the story for Lucas, as if it were a novel, from David's perspective. I'd inhabit his body, feel his longing for Bathsheba, experience his machinations to get her into his bed, perceive his panic over the pregnancy, feel his anxiety to undo his mistake, and suffer the hardening of his heart when he killed her husband. As I sat there, I knew I'd stumbled onto a live-wire story with endless possibilities.

I was so excited to write it that my fingers started to fly over the keyboard. I churned out forty pages in my first sitting. I typed for so long that I got tennis elbow in my forearm. I lost hours of work over the next several days. I would fall asleep dreaming about the story and would wake up thinking about it. Here is what I wrote Lucas.

Dear Lucas,

Preacher Man told you David also killed a man. Well, here's that story through David's eyes.

It was springtime when the desert air was crisp and the sun radiant. My bedroom, which also served as my office, was on the top floor of my palace and had a large patio that overlooked the city of Jerusalem. After sleeping until late in the morning, I went onto the patio, sat on a chair, shut my eyes, and faced directly into the sun, trying to warm my bones.

My men were in battle a day's journey away, overseen by my fine generals, whom I'd raised up and led over the past several years. I'd been right there with them for every battle, every skirmish, shoulder to shoulder and boot to boot. But it had taken a toll on me and now I was attempting to rest and recuperate.

My face began to radiate with the tinge of a burn, so I walked to the edge of the patio and leaned on the iron railing overlooking Jerusalem. My generals all had nice homes, with courtyards and gardens, located just below my palace, and the city sprawled beyond their houses. As I basked in satisfaction, a flash of light caught my eye.

I searched for its source and spotted a woman bathing on her patio. The flash of light was the sun reflecting off her shimmering body. Apparently, she was as anxious to enjoy the spring sunshine as I was.

Facing away from me, she reached to the side of the bathtub, picked up a clay jar filled with water, and poured the steaming liquid over her head and shoulders. It cascaded in ribbons through her long, dark hair, trickled down the small of her back, and flowed over the deep curve of her hips. In what looked like praise, she tilted her head back, gazed into the sky, and sputtered water out of her mouth.

She turned around, reached for another pitcher, tilted her face directly into the sun, and slowly poured the water over her closed eyes. It splashed and streaked down her long neck, glistened on her breasts, and dripped into the pool of water below.

She was gorgeous.

Suddenly, she opened her eyes and turned her head in my direction.

I leaped back from the railing and hunched on the ground, out of sight.

After a few moments, I felt foolish to be cowering on my own patio and I rose to walk around. I moved a chair into place, then repositioned a plant in a small clay pot, but she was all I could think about.

I approached the railing again, but this time hid behind a dwarf orange tree planted in a large terra-cotta pot. Now she was lying in her large basin, soaking in the water. She playfully kicked her feet into the air and then tilted her head toward me. The sun reflected off her gleaming teeth.

Was she smiling at me?

Flirting?

"You fool," I muttered to myself, "she doesn't even know you."

She grabbed the sides of the basin and sat up abruptly, still looking my way. I thought she might have spotted me behind the tree, so I pushed away from the railing and hurried to my bedroom.

Mentally churning, I busied myself by cleaning up my desk. Within seconds, she crashed back into my mind—her glistening body, the curve of her hips, the fullness of her breasts, the rivulets of water through her hair. I yelled out for my scribe to come to me, and I tried to dictate a letter. But all that came out was gibberish. I dismissed him and paced my bedroom, begging God to purge these thoughts from my mind. He didn't. I wrote a psalm about my temptations, but it only brought her into sharper focus. By evening, I was mentally exhausted.

I called one of my servants, described where I'd seen the woman, and asked him to find out who lived in that house. He came back with word that Uriah the Hittite lived there with his wife, Bathsheba. Uriah was one of my finest generals, a loyal soldier in the highest tradition of military service. We had fought many battles side by side.

He also had a stunning wife.

I turned away in disgust that I would even consider engaging the wife of one of my generals. I busied myself with more tidying and talking and *walking, but the rivulets were relentless, undulating like waves down her glistening body.*

I rebuked myself. I shook my head violently to purge the thoughts. I slapped myself. Then I slapped myself again. Then in a fit of maniacal lust, I yelled out for my servant to come.

My body tingled. I wanted this woman; I needed this woman; I couldn't not not have her.

I thought, Maybe if I summon her it will break my fantasizing and snap me back to reality.

"Bathsheba," I said to myself as I waited.

A voice bubbled up from deep inside of me. Queen Bathsheba.

It made no sense. She was just a beautiful woman on a patio—and already someone's wife. In all my years as king, having had many wives before, I had never felt so magnetized by a woman, so utterly tempted, so possessed.

Facing away from my servant, I ordered, "Bring me Bathsheba."

I hesitated, hoping he'd ask me to clarify and I would tell him it was only in jest. I would then ask for some other woman and shield Bathsheba and her marriage from my yearning.

Turning toward him, I called out, "Wait." But he was gone.

Bathsheba came to my darkened bedroom that night. Her shape simply appeared in my doorway. For a moment, my breath caught itself. My heart was pounding. I was shaking. And instantly, there was no war, there was no time, there were no consequences, there were no servants. There was only her.

"Bathsheba," I whispered, still breathless from the sight of her.

"My King," she said, with reverence and tenderness.

Her voice flowed through me like a night breeze. Her thick hair fell in waves. Her silk evening robe seemed to catch the moonlight on her deep curves. I felt drunk in her presence.

"Would you like...some...wine?" I sputtered, a half-grown boy in king's clothes.

"If it please you, my King." Her eyes met mine. She was there out of obedience. But something in her gaze, something in her eyes, told me she knew; she knew what I saw from my terrace; she knew the feelings rumbling inside of me.

But how did she feel?

She accepted some wine, and then some more. She told me about her quiet, empty home. As her tongue loosened, she told me she was married to the sunlight on her balcony, and her home, and her patio. She said her husband was married to war and to heavy silence when he was home. She said his name not once.

It was the middle of the night, but the sun seemed to glow beneath her skin. Her voice melted my thoughts. The wine warmed us both. The air between us began to spin, pulling us toward one another, and I reached for her. She closed her eyes and received my gentle kiss, first on her forehead, then on her soft cheek. My lips hovered near hers. The space between our chests whirled and pulled. Send her away, was my last pleading thought before Bathsheba opened her brown eyes and saw through the core of me. She saw the man, not the king. She saw the shepherd boy, not the slayer of Goliath. She saw the strain on me, the pressure, the weight of the crown. She knew me. Somehow, she knew me like no other woman ever had. I had to be with this woman.

She closed her eyes again and received my mouth onto hers. I felt her lean into me, and I wrapped her into my arms. Her body melted into mine.

In the morning, with very few words, she left, and it was done. It was over. Just this once. No one would ever know.

A month later, my servant knocked on my door with the words, "Bathsheba is pregnant." What? I screamed to myself. Pregnant? I closed my eyes and silent-screamed until my mind's eye was brilliant white.

After catching my breath, I wondered how long Uriah had been gone from her. I found out it was only a little over a month, so there was still time to make him appear to be the father. Now, how to get him home. My mind, spinning like a dervish, came up with the idea to pull him off the battlefield for a briefing in Jerusalem. While he's here, *I thought,* he will have opportunity to sleep with his wife, and then he will seemingly be the father. Problem solved.

Joab, my highest-ranking general and Uriah's commander, was shocked by the order to take Uriah out of battle, but he complied.

Uriah showed up the next day with his head high, chest out, and shoulders thrust back. His face was freshly washed, his beard trimmed in a way that exposed untanned parts of his face, and his clothes were clean, but battle worn. He seemed nervous to be dealing directly with me, but I tried to make him feel at ease. I drew up some fictional military orders for him to deliver to Joab.

Then, after a few awkward minutes, I dismissed him and wished him and his family well. I was certain he would hurry home to see his wife.

But I didn't know Uriah.

As I closed the door, I held the handle and let out a long sigh. All would soon be back to normal, and I could eat and sleep again.

But that night, Uriah did not make love with the most beautiful woman in Jerusalem. He didn't sleep in her bed. He didn't even hold her. No. He slept under the stars, outside the palace gate, on the cobblestones, with only a blanket, resisting his marital privilege, just like his men who were on the battlefield that very night.

In the morning, when my servant told me where Uriah had slept, a chill came over my body. My mind shifted into battle mode. How can I get this man with his wife? How can I reduce him?

Alcohol! That was it. Wine was the great equalizer. Like nothing else, it would reduce men to their base selves and dissolve their resolve. Even an oak like Uriah could be reduced to a mere pine.

I quickly organized a banquet to honor General Uriah. I'd not only ply him with wine, but I'd also add the aphrodisiac of military heroism. Fine food would cross his lips, wine would trickle down his throat, and toasts would be proclaimed in his honor. This grand feast would set the stage for him to enjoy the adoring embrace of his wife.

Uriah did enjoy fine foods; he drank the best wine; he uncomfortably endured the praises of men. But again, he slept alone on the same cobblestones, with the same blanket, alongside the same beggars as the night before. Just like his men in the field.

The next morning, I accepted the news of his sleeping arrangements with a strange calm. I didn't panic; I didn't fret. I knew exactly what to do. I wrote a different order for Uriah to carry to Joab. In my own handwriting, I told him to put Uriah on the front lines of battle and when the fighting was the fiercest, to withdraw all the other men, leaving Uriah exposed to the enemy. I rolled up the parchment, dripped some red wax on the seam, and pressed my insignia into the melted wax.

This was expedience. This needed to be done. For the sake of the kingdom. Yes, the kingdom.

That evening, after I'd closed my eyes to sleep, the day's activities paraded themselves across my mind. I saw the kind of death I'd brought upon Uriah. An ignominious death for a true soldier. Not death by my hand. Not even death by the enemy's hand. But death by desertion. These men were his brothers, they'd sacrificed for each other, and sworn they'd die for each other. His last thought wouldn't be of nobility or brotherhood or sacrifice, but one of shock and bewilderment and betrayal that his band of brothers had turned on him.

I shot out of bed to see if my letter had been dispatched. It was already gone from my desk. Uriah would die and I would be responsible. Joab, his superior, would never respect me again. Bathsheba would be a widow. And the baby would be fatherless.

You would think I'd be racked with guilt. You would think Uriah's death would haunt me and that Joab's disgust would rankle me. But I felt nothing. In fact, not only did the murder not bother me, but after the period of mourning, in my blinding hubris, in my gross arrogance, I took Bathsheba to be my wife. She gave birth to our son.

After a week, he fell seriously ill, and we worried for his life. Nathan, the prophet, unexpectedly came to visit me at the palace, and I thought maybe he'd come to heal my son. He was a sturdy man of God, and I trusted his messages for me and the people. When he arrived at the palace, I went to greet him, looking for a warm hug and a blessing for my son. But instead, he blurted, "David, there were two men in a certain town, one rich and the other poor." He pursed his lips and stared at me.

No hug? No greeting? I thought. That's not how you treat the king. But his glare unsettled me.

Finally, out of deference for the prophet, I played along. "Okay, two men, one rich the other poor. And...?"

This seemed to be what he was looking for, so he continued, "The rich man had a very large number of sheep and cattle, but the poor man had nothing except one little lamb. He raised it, and it grew up with him and his children. It shared his food, drank from his cup, and even slept in his arms. It was like a daughter to him."

I thought, I like this poor man.

"Now a traveler came to the rich man, but the rich man refrained from taking one of his own sheep or cattle to prepare a meal for the traveler. Instead, he took the little lamb that belonged to the poor man and prepared it for the one who had come to him."

"As surely as the Lord lives, the man who did this must die!" I shouted. "He must pay for that lamb four times over, because he did such a thing and had no pity."

I expected Nathan to smile at my righteous indignation, but his eyes only widened, as if he'd been slapped. Then he narrowed his gaze, leaned to within a few inches of my face, and said, "David. You. Are. That. Man."

My mind went blank.

He stepped back and bellowed, "You are that rich man!"

My mind raced. What does he mean? How am I that man?

Nathan spun away from me and paced the foyer, his hands clasped behind his back, his head down, mumbling as he walked. "I anointed you king over Israel. I laid my hands on you." Then he stopped, as if an idea had just dawned on him. "And David, if all this had been too little, I would have given you even more. Why did you strike down Uriah the Hittite with the sword and take his wife to be your own?"

My body flushed and my face was on fire. He knew.

"You killed him, David. And now, now the sword will never depart from your house."

His words were a punch in the gut, and I doubled over. They rang in my ears: "You are that man...you are that man...you are the rich man."

Then, as if in a dream, the events from the past year flew through my mind: the patio, her bath, my bedroom, the banquet, the red wine, the red wax. I had ripped a man's wife from him. I had ripped a man's own life from him. I was that coldhearted rich man ripping the tiny, precious, innocent lamb from the poor man.

Then everything went silent. Instantly, I could see clearly. I whispered slowly but deliberately to Nathan, "I have sinned against the Lord."

I didn't whisper out of indecision or embarrassment or a desire to avoid punishment. No, I whispered out of shock that I had been so blind and so evil and so calloused. I would now take any punishment, any consequence, even if it meant giving up the crown. No, I whispered to Nathan out of utter conviction.

Nathan looked at me with eyes half-opened.

I waited.

In a low voice he said, "The Lord has seen your deep sorrow, and he has taken away your sin. You, David, are not going to die. But because you have shown utter contempt for the Lord, the son born to you will die."

And with that, he spun around, pushed open the door, and hurried away. He didn't say goodbye. He offered no blessing. He strode away with an urgency that smelled of disgust.

It was now dark, and I paced the round foyer for hours, walking in circles, occasionally falling on the floor to cry or moan, only to return to my pacing. When my legs started to ache, I went to the stairs, grabbed the railing, and slowly climbed to my bedroom. As I entered, the light of the moon shone through a window, just like it had that night with Bathsheba. I swallowed hard. This time, the moonlight struck my desk, untouched since writing Uriah's death sentence, illuminating a hardened drop of red wax next to the feather pen. I closed my eyes in shame.

As I stood next to my desk, the pen seemed to call out my name, it drew me to itself. I ignored it, but the pull got stronger. I sat down, and suddenly the pen was in my hand. Then it dipped itself in the glimmering black ink and started to move across the papyrus. Words appeared. Then sentences. Then a full poem.

Have mercy on me, O God, according to your unfailing love.

Wash away all my iniquity and cleanse me from my sin.

Against you, you only, have I sinned and done what is evil in your sight.

Cleanse me with hyssop, and I will be clean; wash me, and I will be whiter than snow.

Create in me a pure heart, O God, and renew a steadfast spirit within me.

You do not delight in sacrifice, or I would bring it.

My sacrifice, O God, is a broken spirit; a broken and contrite heart.

Well Lucas, there you have it. I'm shaking as I end this. Writing it has been mind-altering to me. To inhabit David's body like that, to feel all those things—wow, what an experience. I hope you love reading it as much as I loved writing it.

Like Nathan foretold, in spite of David's pleading, his son died. But David lived; he woke to a new day. He'd made a terrible mistake but found the character and humility to recover from it. And his recovery is one for the ages. Forget Goliath. Forget David's era-defining military victories. It was his full-throated ownership of his mistake that set him apart from other men. It was the texture of his humility that earned him the title, "a man after God's own heart." Think of it: David's lowest moment, it turns out, was his finest hour.

But Lucas, I would be disingenuous if I pretended the parallels in this story were only to you. They apply to me, too. I know you know this, but I've fallen also. Not adultery. But I've lost my footing with God; I've pulled back; I've gone cold. I've let what's happened to you and to our family discourage me to the point that I'm barely hanging on to God. This is painful to admit, but my Bible's got dust on it—actual dust! And the only time I'm exposed to it is a verse-a-day app on my phone. So really, I needed this letter as much as you did. I needed David. I needed David's lowest moment to help me find a heartbeat again with God.

Love, Pops

13

Churchless

L ucas, it turned out, loved the David letter.

Dear Pops,

Man, that letter you wrote on David was interesting. I must admit, though, when I opened it and saw how long it was, I threw it on my bunk and thought I'd read it later. Wow Pops, you can sure write a lot of words—haha! But then I realized I had all the time in the world, so I may as well just read it now. I took it onto my cot, got comfortable, tried to shut out all the yapping around me, and read the entire thing from beginning to end. I could not put that thing down. I mean, seriously, to think that that was David, and that it was in the Bible, just blew my mind.

When you told me about how writing it affected you, and how you've lost your way with God, I must admit, I was shocked. I just didn't know you felt that way. I guess I've been too wrapped up in my own world to see it. And then to think that I've been the cause of a lot of your challenges—man, did I feel like a loser.

But I saw a lot of myself in David, too—you know, his rationalizing, his blindness, his stupidity, his love (or I should say lust) for women—I can relate to all those things. But his recovery was awesome; it was so cool to see. I know you've sent me a lot of stuff, like on Nelson Mandela and that quadriplegic who became a physician, and all those other articles—and they were all great—but I gotta tell you, this David story is my favorite.

Love, Lucas

I was not exaggerating when I said that writing the David letter changed me. It did. Not so much the writing of that specific letter about David, but that by writing it I felt compelled to open my Bible again.

After David, I channeled some other Bible characters like Joseph, Deborah, Solomon, Abraham, and even Adam and Eve. As I immersed myself into each person's life, sliding into their world, occupying their mind, seeing life through their eyes, the Bible started to feel different to me—more real and earthy and raw. One-dimensional characters took on nuance and shape and depth, struggling with decisions, making bad choices, and sometimes drifting from God. I saw that relationship with God was wrestling with God. I also saw that maybe I wasn't as far from God as I thought.

By this point it had been years since I had attended church regularly. After I resigned the ministry when Lucas was a junior in high school, I lasted another year in that church and realized it was time to move on. I still had many friends there, but the heavy-handedness and narrow, self-righteous teaching began to wear on me. Plus, being the ex-leader, skulking like Gollum on the back row got weird and became no fun at all.

At first, I felt incredible relief just to be away from the group that had witnessed my family's implosion. But soon, relief morphed into discouragement. It was not so much discouragement about the ex-pastor and ex-church thing. My real discouragement was with God and what my family's demise said about me as a Christian. I felt like I'd failed at one of the pillars of faith: taking care of your family, raising your kids right, or at least raising them to respect God. To have one son prodigalize, that happens. But at this point, two were already running away from God and Chris was not far behind. How could I even call myself a Christian father?

No matter that I had prayed more for my family than any other single thing over the past fifteen years. No matter that I had thought about it constantly and read, I don't know, fifty books on the subject, and attended no less than a dozen retreats. No matter that I had tried to serve God faithfully and put him first and sacrifice for him. And after all that, after all those years, after all that prioritizing, I thought he would bless my family and bless my parenting. It's not like I expected the Christian version of the Cleavers from *Leave It to Beaver*, but I thought I'd at least have a family that vaguely resembled a Christian family.

What was I supposed to do with such a disconnect? How was I expected to rationalize an outcome like this in my faith, and process a discouragement that was so deep? I didn't know. I didn't want to just stop believing in God; I didn't want to shake my fist at him or curse him or hate him or resent him for not blessing me.

One part of me wanted distance, like a God-sabbatical. Just opening the Bible was painful. Every time I did so I would be swarmed with memories of what I used to be and what I used to hope for and how I used to pray.

But another part of me wanted to stay engaged. Another part of me wanted to migrate to the more melancholy, contemplative, sober parts of the Bible to see if I could find some solace there. Joyce and I must have read Psalms and Job a dozen times. We read a book called *Disappointment with God* and others like it. Then we found Solomon in the Bible. He wrote Ecclesiastes—you know, the meaningless-meaningless-everything-is-meaningless book. (And ironically, he was David and Bathsheba's son, after their first son died.) Here was a guy who spoke our language. Here was a guy who was realistic and honest and thoughtful and, okay, a bit unsentimental and blunt and dour. I'm surprised he's even in the Bible—I think he might have just slipped in during one of the darker days of the fourth-century Councils. I'm sure if they could do it again, they'd leave him out. He's not a guy you hear quoted much in church. His words aren't found on Christian greeting cards. But you sure do hear him quoted by people like us. He spoke to the disillusioned and the disappointed and the discouraged and the spiritually bobbing around. You could read him while staring out at the ocean, on a foggy morning, with tears in your eyes. You could think about his words as you walked on the beach so long that your legs went numb. Here are some of the verses that kept us afloat:

Naked a man comes from his mother's womb, and as he comes, so he departs. Ecclesiastes 5:15

When times are good, be happy; but when times are bad, consider: God has made the one as well as the other. Ecclesiastes 7:14

Sow your seed in the morning, and at evening let your hands not be idle, for you do not know which will succeed, whether this or that, or whether both will do equally well. Ecclesiastes 11:6

This is what I have observed to be good: that it is appropriate for a person to eat, to drink, and to find satisfaction in their toilsome labor under the sun during the few days of life God has given them—for this is their lot. Moreover, when God gives someone wealth and possessions, and the ability to enjoy them, to accept their lot and be happy in their toil—this is a gift of God. They seldom reflect on the days of their life, because God keeps them occupied with gladness of heart. Ecclesiastes 5:18-20

And our favorite:

I have seen something else under the sun: The race is not to the swift or the battle to the strong, nor does food come to the wise or wealth to the brilliant or favor to the learned; but time and chance happen to them all. Ecclesiastes 9:11

As we continued to find our balance with God, the thought of going to church became less and less appealing. We realized that our service in the ministry, our role as deacons, and our immersion in an over-the-top, hands-on church over thirty years had burned us out and left us scarred. We had somehow lost God in the swirl of religion. Like a tree that grows over a chain link fence, doctrines and church attendance and relationships with people and the keeping up of appearances had grown over our simple faith in God, our love for him, and our connection to him. It was all too complicated now, too intertwined, too people oriented. God, and all his bigness and magnanimity, his mystique and transcendence, his Spirit and his still, quiet voice, had become too drowned out, too reduced, too limited by organization, and too quantified by doctrines.

Now I needed a massive reordering of my faith and my relationship with God. I needed space. I needed room. I needed a head-clearing time so I could sort out what in the heck I believed. It was time to rediscover God and somehow separate my religion and my family implosion from my faith.

After several years of rarely attending church, Joyce and I started to feel guilty. Then she reminded me that the Bible says, *Where two or three gather in my name, there I am with them.* Ha! So we were a church. We were a church with no services or official meetings or communion or hymns. We were just two congregants, licking their wounds, trying to keep their heads above water, wearing thin the pages of Solomon and Job.

During this time, however, we would occasionally venture out to visit local churches, usually at the invitation of a friend. It seemed our visits always ended up with us finding a couple reasons—or maybe half a dozen—to dislike the church. One of them had a bombastic, finger-pointing preacher, just like our old church—I left halfway through. Another had a preacher we loved, but the music was ear-piercing rock 'n' roll that was just too much.

One service, in particular, began when the band started playing a familiar hymn, with a rock 'n' roll twist. I loved the hymn, but this rendition was tinny and loud. The female vocalist had a great voice and did the best she could, but I sensed she was tired, maybe having sung this hymn one too many times in her life. I immediately related to the fatigue that comes from repeating something a thousand times, something that may have started out organically but now only reflected a steely determination to do the right thing. Or, well, maybe I was just overthinking it. Maybe she'd just had a long Saturday night.

Then the preacher mounted the stage, and he looked the part: tall, a beard perfectly flecked with grey, folksy—you know, the kind of guy you'd want as a pastor and a neighbor. I tried to be open-minded to his sermon, but he started throwing around preacher jargon, like "theological" and "exegesis" and "hermeneutics." *Come on*, I thought, *people don't use those words. Just talk like a normal person. We don't care that you went to seminary.*

Then he committed the preacher sin I'd seen committed one too many times: he overstepped. When applying a verse from the Bible, he tried to make it say more than it said. And when he did, he morphed from folksy to salesy, and my stomach turned. I think the verse was in Matthew, where Jesus stated a promise: *If you seek first his kingdom, all these things will be added to you as well.* It's a great promise with a clear, "if" and "then." *If* you seek first his kingdom, *then* (in this context) food, drink, and clothing will be added to your life. Fair enough.

But this preacher couldn't leave well enough alone, he had to sweeten the pot. To food, drink, and clothing, he added wealth, health, obedient kids, a happy marriage, and no cancer. I shouted to myself, *That's not what it says, pal! You're trying to sell this too hard and give people false hope. Just let it say what it says! It's an amazing verse.*

I knew when I called the pastor "pal," I was not in a good frame of mind. It was time to just lean back in my chair, take a deep breath, relax my shoulders, lower my eyelids, and travel to my happy place, maybe out on the trail with Mumford.

I left the auditorium as soon as the sermon was over and went to sit in my car while I waited for Joyce. I tilted the seat back, closed my eyes, and thought about the mental gymnastics I had just engaged in. *Can I not even sit through a sermon anymore? Am I that jaded? How can church be my least favorite place to be?* These questions troubled me. I'd fallen so far from my former days. I used to be the one on that stage; I was the one with a Bible in my hand and confidence in my voice. But now I could barely sit through a service; I couldn't stand it when preachers overreached; I recoiled against simplistic, presumptuous, prescriptive sermons. I was questioning everything I had once believed.

14

Reception

About a month after being sentenced, Lucas was transferred to the reception center in Delano, California. It was here that the department of corrections assessed prisoners based on factors such as their criminal, mental, and social history, as well as their level of compliance while in jail and at this facility. This led to a custody score of between one and four, with the highest-risk criminals rating a four. They used this score to match the inmate to an appropriate long-term prison. Lucas was rated a two.

Reception was designed to be a short stay, perhaps as brief as a few weeks. But it could also stretch to six months, especially with California's mushrooming prison population. Lucas's stay turned out to be five months—five long months of waiting with hundreds of other men, all with nothing to do. No programs. No library. No classes. Paltry outdoor facilities. But plenty of playing cards. Lucas told me that some days they would play Texas Hold'em for eight hours. They gambled with jars of coffee, soup, honey buns, deodorant, chips, soda, and, of course, Top Ramen. There were days he won sixty packets of noodles and days he lost sixty.

Shortly after getting to the reception center, Lucas dropped a bombshell: he wrote us that while there he wouldn't be allowed visitors or phone calls, only letters. Yes, our only form of interaction with him would be black marks on a white page. As the months wore on, we became very familiar with envelopes, stamps, and the words, *Reception Center, Delano, California.*

Lucas told me later, though, that the letters became the perfect antidote to the monotony and otherworldliness of that place. They kept him tethered to real life, like those random pictures that show up on your Facebook feed from years ago. He needed constant reminding that it wasn't normal to have thousands of bored-to-death men cooped up in dorms, playing cards all day, talking gibberish, surrounded by razor wire. Every day at about three o'clock, right before afternoon count, the dorm officer would announce who got mail that day. It was one of the highlights of his day, and Lucas said his name was called almost every day. In fact, one of the prison guards pulled him aside and told him that he'd never seen an inmate get as much mail as Lucas did.

Writing frequently to another person, however, can get old real fast. I couldn't muster the energy of a David letter every time, and comments about the triple-digit heat and the latest mountain trek with Mumford—as much of a one-of-a-kind dog as he is—wore thin quickly. But it turned out that I got fresh material to write about when my dad's dementia escalated.

Dear Lucas,

After another month of crazy here in Arizona, I had to do the unthinkable—I had to admit Opa, against his will, to the psych ward. Ugh. Yes, I, his eldest son, his advocate, his last defense against the world, had to deliver him to a lockdown ward at the VA hospital in Tucson. I feared I was being a Judas.

When we arrived at the VA, the reception area to the ward seemed normal. But to gain access to the wing, they opened a large automatic door that looked to be six feet wide. As I turned to watch the door shut behind me, I noticed it was disguised to look like a bookshelf. Hmmm, I thought, that's weird.

The nursing staff greeted us warmly and then separated us for intake interviews. They asked about Opa, how he'd been acting, and what I had done to intervene. When my interview was over, I waited for him in the hallway. Other patients walked by or were wheeled past me. Some drooled, others talked to imaginary people, and others stared catatonically into space. I began to wonder if Opa really belonged here.

Right on cue, Opa came barreling down the hallway and told me to get him the hell out of there. As we stood up to make our getaway, the medical director, a silver-haired lady with a strong German accent, stepped into the hallway and asked me to come into her office. I let Opa know I would just be a minute. The head nurse also joined us and, curiously, left the office door wide open.

I sat in a chair on one end of the room, and they stood together at the other. They asked me for specifics about Opa's antics over the previous couple months. I reached into my back pocket and unfolded a printout of an Excel sheet that listed the dates and details of his sweepstakes misadventures: mailing a hundred thousand dollars in checks, almost punching me at the bank, the surreal Landmark Cafe breakfast, the ghosting of all his friends, and all the rest.

The director crossed her arms and told me rather plainly that Opa needed to stay there for observation. I was a little taken aback by her quick judgment and told her that the other patients seemed so much worse off than he did.

Just then, through the open office door, I saw Opa walk to the middle of the wide hallway, lean forward, and stare at me as if I were a gazelle and he were a leopard. He narrowed his eyes, scrunched his forehead, and seemed to be trying to bore a hole through me. Then, as if someone had called his name from down the hall, he straightened up and started walking in that direction.

I laughed and said, "Well, that's par for the course."

The director and nurse smiled.

I continued, "But I'll be honest, I'm struggling here. I just don't want to put him somewhere before he's ready. I guess what I'm trying to say is that I don't want to leave him at 'the cuckoo's nest' before he's really cuckoo." But as I said that to them, I envisioned what he'd be like if I brought him home: he'd bounce around the cab of that truck, flailing his arms, yelling at me, and swearing that he'd never see a doctor again as long as he lived.

Then Opa did his leopard thing again, this time a little closer to the open office door. He peered into the room, leaned over, and glared at me with that same fire in his eyes, making it crystal clear that he wanted to Thelma-and-Louise it outta there. Then, like before, as if he'd gotten a call from another part of the building, he resumed his pacing down the hall.

The nurse, who had been mostly quiet, spoke up. "Ken, I've been here for a long time, decades now. I've seen a lot of men in your dad's condition, and I want you to know that he's sick. His brain is seriously deceiving him. We see men in his condition all the time. This is what we do here."

She was poised and compassionate and seemed to care about him and about my quandary as his caregiver. I found myself leaning into her words.

Then she hit a nerve. "Trust me, Ken, you should leave him here for observation."

My stomach turned. Trust me? Trust you? I don't even know you. My dad's freaking out here, and you want me to trust you? After mulling over her comment for a few moments, I leaned forward, put my elbows on my knees, and asked, "Tell me, honestly, what would you do if it was your dad?"

She met my gaze for several seconds and then looked down. I could see her purse her lips as she pondered my question.

Lucas, I gotta tell you, it was a moment. I loved that this woman did that. I loved that she thought so hard about what I'd asked. I needed her to put herself in my shoes; I needed her not to treat me like just another family member. I wanted her to imagine that this was her dad.

She lifted her head, looked right at me, and with all seriousness, but with great warmth, said, "If it was my dad, I'd leave him here."

I knew it. I knew she was right. I hated that she was right. I hated that, once again, I had to make a decision based on the least bad option.

After a few torturous seconds, I pointed my thumb out into the hallway and asked how the heck I was going to get out of there with old leopard man stalking me.

The nurse told me they had a hidden door to the outside just to the right of her office, painted to look like a bookshelf. Oh, that's what that was. She told me her staff would distract my dad to another hallway, and I could escape through the secret door. I agreed. After radioing a colleague to draw him away, she leaned out the door, looked left, then right, and motioned for me to follow her. I hurried toward the bookshelf, and it opened magically. I stepped outside into the bright light, looked back, and said, "Thank you. Seriously, thank you very much." She smiled and closed the door.

I found myself standing in an alley no more than seven or eight feet wide, with towering walls, two stories high, on both sides. I was breathing hard and could hear my heart pounding in my ears. What had I just done? Had I abandoned my father when he needed me most? Was I Judas? I looked up at the clear blue Arizona sky and thought about my mom. "Mom," I said out loud, "I don't know what you think about what I just did...Uh, I'm sorry if it wasn't right. I just don't know what else to do."

Lucas, you know Oma. If she was anything, she was gracious. Maybe I'm just wishful thinking, but I think she supported me. She knew how difficult Opa could be.

Opa ended up staying for two weeks. I visited him after the first week, and he tore me a new one. After that disastrous meeting, I wasn't sure what to expect when I went to pick him up. Uncle Gerald was with me and when we first saw him, he was standing in the middle of a hallway looking away from us. He looked so lost, shuffling around like a schoolboy who didn't know how to get home. He greeted us but still had a faraway look in his eyes. After a few minutes of visiting, I went to the pharmacy to see what meds they had him on. The pharmacist said it was just a low-dose antidepressant.

Opa hasn't been the same since. The crazy has disappeared from his eyes. He hasn't even mentioned the word "Mercedes" again, and he's never mouthed the words, two-point-four million either. A week later, I asked him about that number and he got a faraway stare, as if he knew it meant something but just couldn't quite place what it was. It was spooky to watch. His life has become before and after the psych ward, and I struggle with guilt. Was it the drugs? I don't think so. I checked again and it was true, his dose was very low. Was it the trauma of that stay? I don't know. Maybe it was just the natural progression of dementia.

After a few days at home, he still seemed lost, spending most of the day wandering from room to room. On a whim, I suggested he might want to move to an apartment designed for seniors. As the words left my mouth, I thought I might snap at me for suggesting it. But instead, he looked up from the dining room table, smiled, and said, "That's a good idea." I wasted no time, and in ten minutes, we were in the car. Within an hour, we had found a new, clean, Hyatt-level facility where several of his friends also lived.

When I said goodbye to him yesterday, he was nestled in his new little apartment, relaxing in his old brown leather chair, watching TV with the remote in his hand. He seemed so content, so insulated from the outside world, so protected. When he waved goodbye, he had a big smile on his face, and finally seemed happy again. It was like his world had been shrunk to a manageable size and he could finally relax and let his shoulders down. There was no ranch to worry about, no commercial leases to renew, no water pumps or irrigation systems to fix (or, as he called them, irritation systems). Now he had a tiny apartment, a TV, an easy-to-use remote, "chef-inspired" meals at seven, noon, and five with a hundred people his age. Now he could nest.

I felt so good when I closed his door; I felt like I'd done the right thing by him, that this was where he needed to be.

It's funny how circular life is. It starts so small, in a warm, watery womb, and then a crib. Then it expands for sixty or seventy exciting years before it starts to contract and shrink and then shrink some more. I saw it with my mom. She was a woman of the world, making a life on three continents, then traveling all over North and South America in her retirement. Then it was only Arizona, then only Sierra Vista, then only her home, then only half her home, then her bedroom, then finally just her bed, where she passed.

And now I'm seeing the same thing with Opa. Maybe it was good I was here to help him transition; maybe he needed me to shrink his world. I think I did right by him. Maybe I am a good son.

Love, Pops

15

Letters

Before long, I was churning out letters to Lucas several times a week. I told him more about my life than I think he wanted to know. I listed a few new year's resolutions I'd considered, and then told him I didn't make resolutions anymore. I knew that made me a cynical old fart, but I didn't care anymore—which made me even *more* of a cynical old fart.

In another letter, I started telling him about some challenges my sisters and I were having over the care of our dad. I wrote generally, telling him how they didn't seem to appreciate me or the load I was carrying for the family. Then I looked up from my laptop and thought, *Why am I being so general? Why don't I just tell him what's really going on and how I just hung up on my sister and was going to drive back to LA the next morning if she didn't show some acknowledgment for the sacrifices I was making for the family? Come on, he's sitting in this hellhole day after day, bored out of his mind. Give him something juicy to read.* So, I did. I gave him the raw, unfiltered truth (at least how I saw it).

I wrote him about how I was considering a possible promotion at work. It was a management position, which I would *not* have been good at. My growing disdain for bureaucracy and my increasing impatience with people would have made me a terrible manager. But I was letting my ego get in the way. So again, instead of just being vague, I unloaded on him, as if I were journaling, writing my way into clarity, riffing on my job, outlining my strengths and weaknesses, telling him what annoyed me in the workplace. I reflected on my career, the investments I'd made in education, like getting an MBA in my midthirties, and how it had all paid off, but how now that I was older, now that I was set, I was less focused on my career. Now I cared about new things—hobbies, like growing stuff and building stuff and terracing hills and making wine with grapes I'd grown and outfitting a campervan so I could hike deep into the Sierra. I told him how writing was becoming my new love, like my letters to him and journaling my way into mental health. But I did not tell him that I'd had the thought, for the first time ever, that maybe I'd write a book about these letters to him while he was in prison.

And then there was Mumford. In one particularly whimsical writing session, I wrote four pages about my daily, early-morning hikes with the boy, his acrobatic frisbee catching at the park, his surfing of the five-foot waves at Carpinteria Beach, and our treks through the Angeles National Forest. I told Lucas how I'd almost lost Mumford high up in the mountains, when he'd chased a deer in the snow on one freezing night, and then limped around a shrub illuminated by my headlights just as darkness was setting in and the temperature was dropping into the twenties, seconds before I needed to drive away because the pass was closing. And how, minutes before, I'd called his mom (Joyce) and cried like a baby that I'd lost my partner. I think I had Lucas for four pages—he's a dog lover too—but at the end of page four, I knew it was time to wrap up my Mumford infatuation.

I also wrote him more letters like the David letter.

I channeled Joseph when he was imprisoned for refusing to sleep with his boss's wife—a story that had intrigued and upset Lucas as a preteen. It, too, had all the elements of a juicy novel, which I ended by talking about Joseph's miraculous ascension to the highest-ranking man in all of Egypt, second only to Pharoah.

Then I channeled Solomon, the most famous addict in history—one who shared many of Lucas's tendencies toward excess. I recreated the Queen of Sheba scene, where Solomon's wisdom was on full display.

I had fun with Adam and Eve, bringing to life the Garden scene, with one-dimensional Adam and three-dimensional Eve. It gave me the chance to rant on free will and consequences and randomness in the universe. Completely unexpectedly, even though it was channeling just to my son, it helped me crystalize some of my own beliefs about these big ideas. For example, I had long fancied God as a micromanager, meddling constantly in human affairs, but came to see that I didn't believe that anymore.

Then I had to deliver some bad news to Lucas.

Dear Lucas,

I'm so sorry to have to do this in a letter, but something big happened: Opa died. Yeah, I'm sorry you had to find out this way. It happened a couple days ago.

The day before he died, we had lunch at Vinny's New York Pizza, near his retirement home. It was one of his favorite spots, with its red-and-white checkered tablecloths, wooden picnic tables, and pizza by the slice. That day, he ordered two big slices of greasy pepperoni pizza along with two sides of blue cheese dressing. Not just one side, but two—kinda like you would have ordered. And this wasn't just regular old blue cheese dressing. No, it was the thick, oozing kind with big chunks of blue-laced cheese bobbing around. As he ate the pizza, he baptized each bite in the dressing before stuffing it in his mouth. It was so excessive that I asked him if he'd like some pizza with his dressing—just like I've asked you a hundred times! I hate to admit this, but I actually leaned back halfway through lunch and thought, This man is going to have a blue cheese heart attack.

After lunch, I drove him back to his apartment and pulled under the large canopy that served as the entrance. Normally, I would have just dropped him off, but this time I got out of the truck and met him at the tailgate. I opened my arms to give him a quick Pops-I-enjoyed-lunch embrace, but when I leaned back to let him go, he clung to me. As he held on, I realized it was purposeful—he was trying to tell me something. I returned his embrace, and after several seconds, he let go. Then he grabbed my shoulders, stared up at me from his shrunken five-foot-six frame, his blue eyes reflecting the Arizona sky, and said, "Son, thanks for that. Thanks for taking me to lunch."

I shrugged, not thinking much of it, and said, "Sure, Pops, no problem."

Then he grabbed my shoulders again and held me in front of him. His grip was iron, his smile was gone, but his eyes were still warm and watery. He jutted out his army colonel chin and said more deliberately, "Seriously, champ, that meant a lot to me, so thank you."

I relaxed into his grip when I realized he was really trying to tell me something. I looked intensely into his eyes and said, "Dad. You. Are. Welcome. It was great, yeah. I really enjoyed hanging out together."

He kept staring up at me as if he wanted to say more, his mouth seeming ready to move, but no words came. Then, his eyes got cloudy, and a troubled look came over his face, as if he'd lost his train of thought. It was sad to witness. In an instant, he transformed from bold colonel to insecure recruit. I tried to coax him along and prompt him, but his mind just wouldn't cooperate. We soon hugged, and I made my way back into the truck.

Sitting behind the wheel, before turning the key, I smiled to myself about his uncharacteristic show of warmth and gratitude. Normally, he would have never been that expressive or hugged me that way. But this day he had; this day he'd been overcome with gratitude. And as I sat there, looking out from under the canopy into the bright afternoon sun, I remembered that just months before, I had made the excruciating decision to leave him at the VA. He'd called me things no dad should ever call a son—I thought we were through, and I feared he'd never speak to me again. But it didn't happen that way. Instead, he'd leaned into me, embraced me, and was the most affectionate he'd ever been with me. I realized right then that I'd made the right decision in caring for him—he knew he had someone in the world looking out for him.

The next afternoon, after working at his ranch all day, I called to see if he'd like to do dinner. He didn't answer, so that night I just went to my favorite Thai restaurant on my own. As I sat down, I noticed a message from him. I pressed play and this is what I heard:

"Hello Ken, this is your dad. Uh. I need for you to come here immediately, please. I have a cold sweat; I think I'm having a heart attack or something. But anyway, get here as quickly as you can cuz I'm just—it's got me scared a little bit. Thanks. Bye."

I looked at the timestamp and it said 4:58 p.m., which was about two hours earlier. I bolted out of the restaurant to his apartment. His door was unlocked, and I hurried to his bedroom door. When I turned the corner, I saw him sprawled faceup on the bed, his right arm across his stomach, and his left arm dangling off the bed. Moving closer, I saw that his eyes were open and his head was slightly turned to the side, with a stream of oatmeal-like stomach contents spewing out of his mouth. He'd had a massive heart attack.

I panicked and ran downstairs to find the building manager. As I told him what happened, I broke down in tears and could barely get a word out. He comforted me and took care of things from there.

Maybe an hour later, after the paramedics had left and while a policeman was filling out paperwork, I told the officer I needed a few minutes alone with my dad. I went into his bedroom, shut the door behind me, and stared at him lying on his bed, wondering why I'd needed this time with him. The room was stuffy, with the faint smell of urine in the air, and it reminded me of some of our recent awkward talks about hygiene.

I walked to the far side of his bed, knelt down, and put my left hand on his right forearm, which was now by his side. His eyes were closed, his mouth was cleaned, and his head was propped up by a pillow. His skin seemed suddenly older, littered with liver-colored age spots, and it seemed to hang more loosely on his bones.

I said, "Dad," and immediately felt awkward in the silent, echoey room.

After a few seconds, I tried again. "Pops, thanks. Thanks for the life you gave me, the life you gave us, how you took us all over the world, and gave us an interesting life."

Saying these things felt good and right, like maybe that's why I was in that room.

"And Pops, thank you for your service; you were a true patriot. But even more than that, even more than your willingness to lay down your life for our country—what you did for Mom in her final years, the way you took care of her, you were amazing. So thank you."

Lucas, I hadn't planned on saying any of these things, but very much on my mind was the saint he'd been to Oma. If he'd done nothing else good in his life—no good deeds, no service, no helping others—the way he took care of his wife in her final years would have been enough to make up for a life of nothingness. As her motor neurons ceased working because of ALS and her body slowly deteriorated before his eyes, he cared for her as if she were himself.

Kneeling there, looking at his face and thinking about the past several years and how he'd pulled away from us, I felt a different kind of stirring in my gut. I started to feel agitated and angry, and out of nowhere, I blurted out, "But Pops, you could be a real asshole sometimes, you know that!"

After almost yelling the word "asshole," I stopped, shocked that I'd raised my voice like that. But in that instant, I knew exactly why I was in that room.

"Why didn't you try more with us? It was like you didn't care. Did you? Did you even care about us?" I stared at his face as if I wanted him to answer. "It was like after Mom died you just gave up, you forgot about us, and you crawled into your own little world. What was that about?"

I looked down at the bed as I thought about how he'd treated my two sisters. "And the way you treated Denise and Diane, the way you disrespected them and changed everything Mom set up for them. You knew better than that! And it wasn't just them, it was like each of us had disappointed you, and you just couldn't get off that memory. You'd play that same stupid tape every time you saw us. Every freaking time. I mean, come on, Dad!"

I was breathing hard by now and, no joke, I thought his chest rose—it looked like he'd inhaled a deep breath. I yanked my hand off his forearm and stared at his face. Had he just breathed? I looked at his chest, then his face, then his chest again. There was no movement.

When I realized my imagination was running away from me, I leaned back on my calves and laughed at myself for thinking that he'd pull a Lazarus on me. Man, did I feel stupid. I thought, Come on Ken, the man is dead, and he still has you second-guessing yourself. Wouldn't that be a great headline: "Dead man wakes up to son spilling the family beans and clocks him with a left hook."

After my heart rate slowed, which took a while, I put my hand back on his forearm to continue my little farewell speech. But as soon as I did, I knew the momentum was lost. There were no more words in my heart, Lazarus had sucked them all out of me. I think I eked out a few more pathetic, stilted words, but it just didn't come together. I laughed at myself again, leaned forward, and said, "Pops, I do love you. Goodbye."

Now come on, Lucas, is that not crazy? Why in the world did I need to say those things to my dad? I don't really know, but that was exactly how I felt, and maybe I just needed to get it off my chest. I'd been so disappointed with him, in our relationship and in how he'd been with all of us since Oma died. He'd gone AWOL. It just could have been so much more, so much better, and now it was all over.

And son, as I tell you this, the parallel is not lost on me. I desperately don't want you grabbing my forearm like that when I die. I don't want you to have words unsaid or feel disappointments or resentments about our relationship.

Please, please, please, don't have a speech like that for my cold, lifeless body. I would die. Well, I'd already be dead, but you know what I mean.

Look, I know we've been through hell together, but maybe now things can be different. Maybe this whole crazy experience you've been through, and this letter-writing mania we've been on, can be the start of something new for us. And can I be so bold, can I go out on a limb here? Maybe we can even have something amazing, something few fathers and sons ever have. Maybe the darkness we've seen can bring us a special, unique kind of light.

I pray that one day when you grab my cold forearm, it will be to just say, "Thanks Pops," and, "See you in heaven."

Love, Pops

Dear Pops,

Man, it was sobering to get that letter about Opa dying. I was lying on my bed last night, thinking about you and your dad's relationship. He didn't leave you with the fondest memories, and I'm sorry for that.

I've been in here for over a year, and I've had a lot of time to think about our relationship and the family we had. So many men in here either don't know their father or they hate him for not being there for them. Or sometimes they hate him for being there and doing the things he did to them. I mean, almost everyone's got some complaint. But when I listen to them, I can't relate. I just nod as if my dad was that way, too.

In a way, it makes me feel even worse for being in this place. My family didn't suck. You didn't leave us or beat us or humiliate us. I had a great mom and brothers who loved me. I've got no excuse for why I'm in here.

I spent an hour on that bed thinking of the things you did for me and the brothers. That stupid, most-treasured-possession keep-away game with the rolled-up sock. (I have never wanted something as much as that smelly sock.) And your basketball drills, always forcing me to drive left so I would improve my left-handed dribbling. At the time, I hated you for that (not really), but hey, now I've got a pretty good left hand.

I could go on about other things, but I guess what I'm trying to say is, thank you! I know I haven't often shown it but sitting here in this place has made me see my life in an entirely different light. It's made me grateful for what you gave us.

Love, Lucas

I sat at my desk with his letter in my hands and wept. It felt like all those years of disappointment and dismay and uncertainty and feelings of failure flowed out of my eyes. He *had* noticed. He *did* remember. And maybe, just maybe, we'd be a normal father and son again one day.

There, I'd said it; I had hope again. 'Hope that there'd be hope' had now, for the first time in years, morphed into actual optimism. I admitted to myself, without equivocation, without waffling, that normalcy may be mine again one day.

This letter in my hands felt like a sign, like a smoke signal rising from beyond a distant hill, the white clouds lilting in the air, hanging there, broadcasting a message that over there, over beyond that hill, there was possibility. Those dangling clouds kept me at my desk, tapping away, and printing letters.

I think this resurrection of hope was made possible because Jess had boomeranged from his reckless days. By this point, he'd finished college and was teaching middle school at the same school he'd gone to as a preteen—which, of course, was a delicious irony, given the hellion he'd been when he'd attended. His wife, Nicole, was beautiful inside and out and worked as an ICU nurse. Their towheaded son had been born a year before, right around the time of Lucas's accident. They'd bought a house only five minutes from ours, and we saw each other several times a week, enjoying meals and playing basketball on our court. In a moment of irony, Jess laughed that we'd become his favorite people to hang out with. And his rebound from near felon to where he was today, and where *we* were today, lingered in my mind as I held onto Lucas's letter. *Could this happen with Lucas? Could it?*

Jess was the older brother in the literal and emotional sense. He looked out for his brothers. He'd visited Lucas at County and spoken to him on a level I just couldn't. The advice from Jess that Lucas had mocked or squandered when he was abusing substances was now like gold to him. I'm not sure they ever chimed in together on a Tupac song, but I suspect they might have joked about it a time or two.

Chris, on the other hand, was still wrestling with his own opioid addiction. Four years in the Navy had been good for him, but as soon as he returned, he fell back into old patterns. His addiction wasn't crazy, with him stumbling around the house, but it did cause him to become a hermit. He would just hunker down in his bedroom with his door closed and play video games all hours of the day and night. And he could do that because he was living with us—which, of course, became a problem, just like it had with Lucas. I had hoped Lucas's arrest, and the role Chris played in it that night when he drove him to the police station, might scare him straight. But it didn't. It actually seemed to do the opposite; it seemed to draw him deeper into himself—further away from normalcy. While living with us, he became completely unreachable, even to Jess.

But Lucas's letter and Jess's turnaround had me believing that recovery was possible. It could actually happen. And it could even happen with Chris.

16

California Rehabilitation Center

After five long months in the giant holding tank of Reception, Lucas was assigned to a permanent facility in Norco, California, about thirty miles east of Los Angeles. It was called the California Rehabilitation Center (CRC) and was about ninety minutes from our home.

The prison's stated goal is rehabilitation. And for a small percentage of the thousands of inmates, it was just that—a place for them to rebuild their lives. But because of overcrowding, most of the inmates assigned to CRC had no interest in changing. These inmates were assigned to "nonprogramming" buildings, which housed eighty men in two large rooms, with twenty bunk beds on one side and twenty on the other. It was a population density that made college dorms look roomy. Lucas was initially assigned to one of these buildings, and the close quarters were making him crazy. He told me the chattering was incessant, starting early in the morning and continuing into the night, grown men milling around, purposeless, telling jokes (usually sexual), playing music, watching TV, working out, playing pinochle, and shamelessly bragging about their life on the "outs."

The different racial groups—white, Black, Mexican, and "other"—each had their own Men's Advisory Council rep (MAC), who would speak on their group's behalf. Because race was the simplest distinction among inmates, it became the primary differentiator. Each of them having a rep was the only way to keep things under control. Lucas shared a bunk at the end of the room with the Black MAC and became good friends with the white one. This association helped him to steer clear of trouble.

When we visited CRC, we'd fill out some personal information on a small Post-it-sized sheet of paper and submit it to the guards with our driver's license paper-clipped to it. Then we'd join a dozen other people sitting on benches—or pacing, like me—and wait for our name to be called. As I meandered, I would often look through the chain-link fence, up the hill to the prison barracks, wondering how I ended up here, how I'd learned the rhythms and moods of a place so tight and strict and oppressive. It was a place with rigid rules which were meticulously listed but randomly enforced; it was a place where guards could be gracious one visit and gruff the next; it was a place where they'd refuse a visit because your shirt was the wrong color, even though you'd worn that exact shirt on a previous visit. Even though the facility sat a mere five hundred yards from the sleepy suburb of Norco, where couples strolled and children played, it felt like an alternate universe, a world unto itself. It felt Soviet, with its edgy authoritarianism and blunt physicality.

After our name was haltingly mispronounced, "Goo-ed-rose," like a million times before, we were frisked and told to climb fifty stairs to another chain-link fence. This one was threaded through with pale-yellow plastic slats to provide privacy. We unlatched the gate and entered an outdoor patio with about thirty wooden or concrete picnic tables scattered about. Each was numbered and had a large umbrella placed into a center hole for sun protection. We carried our signed paper form, along with a ziplock bag filled with one-dollar bills and quarters. Once we'd checked in with the guard in the reception building, we were assigned a table for our visit.

The reception building was packed with people shuffling around, shoulder to shoulder, jockeying for position in front of vending machines or one of the two microwave ovens. The atmosphere was boisterous, like a large family reunion, with visitors and inmates talking excitedly while they waited in line. The inmates were allowed to mingle with the visitors but were strictly prohibited from touching any money or the snack machines. The room smelled like a cross between

In-N-Out and KFC. Behind the vending glass was every imaginable food: microwavable burgers, turkey sandwiches with provolone, cheese dips, chicken Caesar salad, fruit bowls, and more kinds of chips than I knew existed in the known universe. Then the most popular item of all: a large, greasy, ziplock bag of fried chicken. It didn't appeal to me, but it smelled heavenly. For inmates who were accustomed to bland, colorless institutional food, this place deserved a Michelin star. Oh sure, catching up with loved ones was important, and seeing a son or daughter was significant. But the food, oh the glorious food. Lucas told us that the first and only question his friends asked him when he returned from a visit was, "Whadya eat?"

The first time I visited Lucas after my dad's memorial service, I was anxious. Joyce had seen him the week before, but this would be the first time I'd be face-to-face with him in six months. So much had happened between us over those months, so many letters, so many words, so many confessions, and my dad had passed away. I wasn't sure what it would feel like to be together. It felt like meeting a pen pal for the first time.

There was a small part of me that wanted our relationship to forever be on paper; it was so much easier that way, so much cleaner and simpler, and, in a way, deeper. I knew this was a silly notion, but distance and letters had repaired so much, I didn't want face-to-face to wash it all away.

Lucas walked down the stairs to the patio with a toothy smile and strode toward me in his prison blues and heavy boots. He was slimmer than he'd been at County, and his dark beard was thicker but still well trimmed. I hugged him and could feel from his embrace that he had missed me. After several seconds, I let go, grabbed both sides of his face, and pulled him close so I could get a good look. He let me, and chuckled and grinned as I gazed into his eyes. Yes! Yes! Yes! His eyes were clear and calm.

"Pops, it's good to see you."

"You too, my man."

We found our assigned table, and caught up on family news. After a while, I said, "So, how does it feel knowing me better than your brothers do after all those confessional letters I sent you?"

"Well, you definitely laid it out there, Pops," he laughed, "I'll give you that. Yeah, that was trippy when I started getting those letters from you. You told me all about your dad and that promotion you almost got. And then, when you started telling me about your life, wow, I just wasn't sure what to think."

"Well, as you know, I'm allergic to small talk," I said, "and if I was going to write you a few times a week, I had to tell you something."

"No, I know. Once I understood what you were doing, it started to make sense, and I even tried to do it myself—you know, be more open and honest. But it felt weird at first, and I threw away a bunch of letters. But then it kinda got under my skin, and I liked the feeling of, you know, opening up and all."

"Yeah, I could tell you were enjoying it," I said, "and it seemed like you really got into a groove. I think I was as surprised as you were. I even noticed that your vocabulary started to change and the way you put things seemed, I don't know, just different."

"I also started reading a lot," Lucas said, "and I think that helped. There was this lounge in the reception center, and it had this little table with books on it. I picked up one by James Patterson, and a guy I knew told me it was a good one. So I sat down right there and started reading it. Pops, I'm not lying, I sat there for two hours before I even realized I was reading a book. I was so immersed in the story that, really, for the first time in a year, I felt like I was released from here, like I was transported to a different world, a world that didn't have control of me, you know, didn't have its clutches in me."

"So *that's* what happened! I knew it. It seemed like you'd gotten an injection in your brain. I just had no idea it was James Patterson."

"Yeah, and the more I read, the more my mind got going. I just couldn't get enough. I started sleeping better; my dreams became more vivid; I got eager to get up in the morning. I mean everything changed."

Lucas and I went to a vending machine to buy some fresh-cut mango and as we returned to our table, I took note of some of the people around us. One table had a muscle-bound, tatted-up man visiting quietly but intensely with a woman. They had a Bible between them, which they would rotate so the other could read it. Next to them was a table of two adults and two kids. They played board games supplied by the prison while munching on a bag of chicken. When Lucas placed the crisp sliver of mango in his mouth it crunched, and he moaned as his cheeks tightened to the tangy fruit. I smiled. Fresh fruit was like steak to him.

After visiting for another half hour, Lucas leaned forward, put his elbows on the picnic table, and in a fashion I was starting to get used to, he peppered me with personal questions. He asked about my job, about Mumford, about my dad's memorial, about my siblings, and about my hikes in the mountains. He'd shown this kind of assertive interest from his early days at County and maybe a half dozen times since. Each time, though, it seemed beside the point, like he was trying to remove the spotlight from himself, almost like we were ignoring this big fat elephant standing in the middle of the room. But this time it felt different; this time it felt more genuine and fitting. This time we weren't ignoring the elephant in the room—or perhaps I was the elephant in the room. I thought, *If he wants to know about my life, I'll tell him.*

As I talked, he listened intently, and leaned back and smiled with a calmness I'd never seen in him. It lingers in my mind because his relaxed, amused, inquisitive face was such a contrast to our surroundings. He had on a blue V-neck T-shirt with CDCR (California Department of Corrections and Rehabilitation) on the back in huge block letters. He had to sit on the side of the table facing the guard station so he could be watched. Razor wire was spiraled on top of the ten-foot-high chain-link fence behind him. And here he was, smiling at me, listening to me, interested in me, his dad. This was good. This was healthy. I'll remember that smile as long as I live.

As we said goodbye, Lucas said, "Hey, a guy I play basketball with just told me about a job as porter for some of the outside buildings. That's where they hold college classes and where the counselors have their offices. He said I could probably get the job. I think it's janitorial, you know, cleaning bathrooms, detailing golf carts. Oh, and it pays."

"Really? How much?"

"Sixteen cents an hour," he laughed. "But mostly it gets me out of my dorm; it buys me peace and quiet. The guy said it's the best job in here, so I'm dying to see if I get it."

I wished him luck.

17

Dostoevsky

L ucas landed the janitorial job—a job he would have done for free just to get away from the noise eight hours a day—and earned a whopping $6.40 a week.

On my next visit with him, he told me about a fight that nearly broke out in his barrack that morning. "Yeah, one dude left a sock on another guy's driveway."

"Driveway?"

"Oh, that's the space between the bunks. It kinda becomes your little turf, and some guys get really possessive of it, and clean it and polish it, and some even outline it with tape. They get so neurotic that if you touch their driveway, even if your sock falls on it, they'll fight you over it."

I thought about it and said, "In a way, I'm not surprised. It's probably one of the small things in their life that they can control—I can see how they'd feel."

"No, I agree, and it scares me cuz I'm kinda becoming OCD myself. The longer I'm in here, I see my mind drifting that way. I just gotta get outta that building."

I nodded.

"Oh, for that new job I told you about, they gave me a little office. Well, not really an office, more like a closet for my cleaning supplies. But it does have a desk and chair in it, so I've started checking out books from the library and, man, I just love being able to read in quiet. It's a slice of heaven."

"Yeah, I've noticed you've been writing to us more, too. I'm loving those long letters—you know, the ones on that legal-sized yellow paper—with all the quotes from the books you're reading. Man, I've never seen you so focused."

Prop 57 had made possible the kind of mental stimulation Lucas was enjoying. CRC offered inmates college courses, counseling, Alcoholics Anonymous, jobs, trade apprentice programs, church services, and a library full of books. The goal was to help them experience the endorphin release that comes with learning and expanding your mind. If inmates could experience this kind of personal growth, the thinking went, then maybe they'd never return to a correctional facility. In a way, the prison system developed a reverse loyalty program: earn credits and shrink your stay. Each credit, whether a class completed or a meeting attended, shaved a day or a week off one's sentence, and could reduce prison time by months or even years. Surprisingly, few inmates took advantage of the program.

Lucas, however, embraced it like an immigrant embraces the American Dream. He took every course he could, tutored other inmates, worked in the "Lit Lab" (the library), went to Alcoholics Anonymous meetings, and to every church meeting he could. He took college courses, got two associate degrees, and studied harder than he ever had. He sent me one of his term papers with his professor's note at the top: *Your level of thinking and engagement in writing is outstanding. You should definitely consider going back to get another degree. It sounds like your first degree was a "let me get through this."*

About this time, he also wrote, *I just heard some great news today! For sure, I only have to serve thirty-three percent of my sentence because of Prop 57. I can't believe it! My total time served may be as short as three years.*

All the rehab programs in prison definitely helped Lucas. But his real rehabilitation came from something else: a massive reboot of his brain through reading. Yes, plain old reading. James Patterson kicked it off at Reception, but soon it migrated to biographies, memoir, non-fiction and novels. He told me about Malcolm X, who read constantly when he was in prison, either in the library or on his bunk, even into the wee hours of the morning, crouched down next to the bars of his cell, where he'd read from the light of the hallway.

Lucas read Dumas and Dostoevsky, from which he mailed me long passages. I could barely read them without my mind wandering. *Is this my son?* He devoured books by Hemingway, Frankl, Steinbeck, Vonnegut, and C.S. Lewis.

Lucas's transformation wasn't quick or dramatic; it was simply a gradual uptick in confidence and vocabulary and thinking. When I visited, we would walk and talk on a narrow strip of grass about ten feet wide and seventy-five feet long that ran along the chain-link fence on the entrance side of the visiting patio. We paced that strip so many times that we wore a path in the crabgrass. We discussed faith, fairness, science, God, AA, guilt, the universal moral law, and second chances. Once, we got so tired from walking that we stopped to stand for a few minutes, until a guard came up to us and told us that standing wasn't allowed. Pacing was okay but standing wasn't. Uh, all right.

He wrote me the following letter after finishing Dostoevsky's five-hundred-page, densely written novel, *Crime and Punishment*.

Dear Pops,

I finished reading the book last night at midnight. It took me three weeks, and at times it was painfully mundane, overly descriptive, and flat-out boring. But last night it was worth every minute. Raskolnikov, the main character, also killed someone and got ten years in prison, like I did. But his was a Siberian prison—a very different place than CRC to be sure.

The book spoke to me in words I could never have found. Here are some of my favorite sections:

"But to those on this side of the enclosure [prison], that world seemed like some unattainable fairyland. Here was our own world, unlike anything else, here were our own laws, our own dress, our own manners and customs, here was the house of the living dead, a life like none other upon earth."

"I remember those long, tedious days as being as monotonous as the dripping of water from the roof after rain. I remember that it was only a passionate desire for resurrection, for renewal, for a new life that strengthened my will to wait and hope. And in the end, I did grow stronger: I waited, I counted off each day and, even though there were still a thousand of them left, I marked them

one by one with satisfaction...escorted each, buried it and at the beginning of each new day felt glad that there remained not a thousand days, but only 999."

"But here begins a new account, the account of a man's gradual renewal, the account of his gradual regeneration, his gradual transition from one world to another, his acquaintance with a new, until now completely unknown reality. It might make the subject of a new story—but our present story is ended."

Dad, I had tears streaming down my face when I finished the book. I turned off my reading light, closed the book, and laid it on my chest. It was dead silent, everyone was asleep, and I just stared at the ceiling, thinking about my life.

Like Raskolnikov, I felt like Lazarus. I too had died because of my crime; I too felt like I was being raised back to life; I too felt the gradual transition from one world to another.

It was such a strange feeling, to be completely overwhelmed but completely content. I am at peace with where I am, with who I am, with why I'm here, and what my life is becoming.

As I lay there, I felt a peace I'd never felt.

Few things have been able to do that to me. Monte Cristo did. And God does.

Love, Lucas

I received his letter in the early fall of 2018. The sun was beaming through my large south-facing window, lighting up the white tile bar where I sat in the kitchen. I closed my eyes and could picture Lucas on his rack, in the darkness, the clamor and physicality of prison mercifully silenced for the night, the book on his chest, his eyes awash in tears, envisioning himself born again—like Raskolnikov. Hot, salty tears filled my eyes as well. I felt like I was there with him, like I could reach out and touch him lying on his bed. I breathed in deeply and found myself relaxing into the hope he was feeling.

I think that was the moment that Carlo had predicted all those years before: a moment when Lucas would see that ray of light; that moment when the darkness would be pierced, and the moment when a new feeling would flutter in his heart. Could Dostoevsky and Lazarus and Raskolnikov and Monte Cristo and God be that sliver of light?

18

AA

On one of our visits, we sat at a table on the patio, and I asked Lucas how his AA meetings were going.

He replied, "Yeah, no, I'm not really going anymore."

"Really, what's up?" I asked, as I felt a churning in my stomach.

"I don't know, I just don't find 'em helpful. You know, the guys just share the same story over and over. It's really boring, to be honest with you."

I wanted to blurt out, *Already? You're bored? You were bored before and look where it got you.* But I held my tongue.

He looked at me warmly under the shade of the umbrella. "It's just that I get so much more out of classes and reading these books I've found. In those meetings, my brain is in neutral. But when I'm reading, it's going crazy, I'm thinking new thoughts, and creating all these new ideas."

It brought back a question I'd recycled a hundred times: *What does true change look like? What is recovery? What will rehabilitation look like for Lucas?* I was sitting in the middle of a prison complex with the word *rehabilitation* in its name. But was it working? Were these men changing? Was Lucas?

Is recovery when you commit to a program like AA? Well, yes, for many people I know it has been a lifesaver. Is it when you reboot your brain by reading and education? Yes, it's been done. Is it when you are born again spiritually? For sure, I've seen it many times. Or maybe recovery can be sitting at a bar at closing time, studying your bill, realizing how much money you waste on alcohol each week and deciding, on that very barstool, that you will never drink again. For one man I know, that's exactly what happened—and he never did drink again. Might it be when a man digs through his past in therapy in order to recast his demons? Yep. Or maybe it's when a man realizes he has a mental disease and adopts a regimen to level his brain chemistry? Absolutely.

I guess it could be all those things. Or some. Or maybe just one of them.

In my experience, there does seem to be one common thing in everyone I've seen change: the change comes from within. I know this is no grand insight or particularly helpful, but to the great frustration of loved ones, churches, and programs, without internal desire, nothing else matters. All the meetings in the world, inspiring sponsors, insightful therapists, cutting-edge pharmaceuticals, dynamic churches, and life-changing books will not make a difference if the person doesn't genuinely want to change.

"Luke, I don't know, this makes me nervous. Don't you think you should stick with it for a while? I mean, I know the meetings are repetitive, but you know, you're just coming out of this fog, and it's all so fresh."

"No, Dad, I understand how this looks. This addiction thing was a real problem for me, I know that. And sure, I'll go to a few more meetings. But I want you to know that I just don't think AA is going to be my thing, you know, for the long term."

I felt uncertain, yet comforted that he seemed to have his head on straight.

On the drive home that day, though, I worried about his future and fretted over the possibility of a relapse. I remembered him blacked out, sprawled out on the bathroom floor, his head having barely missed the edge of the toilet. I worried I would see him like that again.

These questions of rehabilitation, recovery, and sobriety haunt me even to this day. Why can't there be clearer answers? Why can't the course of therapy be as predictable and certain as treating, let's say, high cholesterol? Maybe the truth is that there are a thousand versions of recovery. Or a million. Or maybe as many versions as there are addicts.

I had to remind myself that this wasn't my battle, this wasn't my demon. I couldn't control my son, and I had one job here and only one job here: to come to peace with what I could *not* control.

This discussion with Lucas made me reflect on how I had handled his addiction as a dad. I was not the kind of parent who meddled or pestered or became enmeshed in his kid's addiction. And it made me wonder if I'd been too laissez-faire? Maybe I should have intervened more. Maybe I should have been more assertive. When I compared myself to other parents of addicts, I was mealy.

What prompted this self-doubt was a book I'd read called *Beautiful Boy* by David Sheff. In it, Sheff, the dad, witnessed his son's descent into methamphetamine addiction. As he tried to help his son, he became entangled in his son's problems and threw his whole life into trying to help him. Sheff forced his son into rehab, corralled him into family counseling, staged interventions, and worried incessantly. In a way, he became addicted to his son's addiction. Sheff became so stressed that it probably caused a cerebral hemorrhage he suffered during this time. When I read about his passion and immersion and commitment to his son, I felt insecure and puzzled, like I hadn't done enough.

I never went to an Al Anon meeting (for the family members of an addict) or initiated any family therapy. I never learned the street names of opioids or mastered the skill of assessing the pupil size of a person who was high. I never commiserated with other parents of the addicted or went to any meetings.

And it's not something I'm proud of. I just didn't—and I wondered what it said about me as a dad. Why didn't I dedicate my life to the addiction more? Why didn't I learn more? Why didn't I go to meetings? I don't know. I had a kid who was an addict—two kids, actually.

Was it because I didn't want to get my hands dirty? I don't think so. Sure, I resisted my life being swallowed up by Lucas's addiction, but I'm not averse to dirty hands.

Was I a Jesus-is-my-vaccine guy? Nope. I believe in meetings and programs, and I'll use any medicine or therapy or book or anything else that will help me or others.

Was I just too selfish? Had I withdrawn too far into myself to even care anymore? No. I still cared. Deeply.

After thinking about this for years, and journaling about it for hours, and talking about it endlessly with Joyce, I came up with the one thing I thought it could be: fatigue. Yes, plain old exhaustion. Not physical burnout, but more emotional, psychological, and spiritual weariness.

I think it was the thirty years I spent in a hypersocial church, where I went to thousands of meetings, sat through thousands of hours of other people talking about their demons, read a library of books on change and parenting, took dozens of classes, and sat through hours of personal counseling, which we called "discipling." By the time Lucas was in his midtwenties, I was just done; I didn't want to hear any more blather. I don't think a straitjacket could have forced me to sit through an AA meeting. I think that's the closest I can get to explaining why I didn't do what Sheff did for his son.

In my own Serenity Prayer sort of way ("Grant me the serenity to accept the things I cannot change"), I had surrendered to that which I couldn't change or control. I'd waved my white flag and come to accept any future. If Lucas chose to ruin his life, that was his choice. In a very real way, I'd given him over to the universe, or to God, or maybe just to himself.

This discussion with Lucas also got me wondering about parenting as well. Had I done the same thing? Had I not done enough? Which, of course, begs the question, how much can we really do as parents? Do we really determine how our kids turn out? Of course, anyone with a track record like mine would ask himself this—no, actually he would torture himself with it. But regardless, was it my fault my sons struggled as they did? Or, if not my fault, was I a major contributor? These questions have dogged me for twenty years, and as Lucas sat in prison, I still didn't have clarity.

Part of the reason I struggle is the wide range of outcomes I've witnessed in parenting of all types. I've seen a short-tempered mom, one who screamed incessantly at her daughter, raise one of the calmest, sweetest young ladies I've known. I've seen a strong Christian leader pander to his toddler, creating a spoiled, entitled kid I would have sworn would become a schoolyard bully. Well, that kid became one of the most gracious, kind, grateful adults I've ever known. I've seen free-range parents raise conscientious, motivated, hardworking kids. I've seen tiger moms raise lay-arounds or provoke rebellion in their kids. Much like with recovery, there seemed to be very few correlations and certainly no silver bullet. So what exactly is good parenting?

When I looked to the Bible for answers, I was shocked, because it says surprisingly little about the subject. Sure, it speaks volumes about how to be a good person and we assume that being a good person will make you a good parent. (Just as being a bad person will probably make you a bad parent.) But it says astonishingly little about the actual act of parenting. And for something so important in life, something that fills entire sections of bookstores, about which there are thousands of podcasts and TV shows, you'd think there would be more than a few verses in the Bible. Out of the 783,000 words in the Good Book, only a hundred or so directly address the subject, and most of those are very general. Why would that be?

Well, here's a thought. Maybe parenting style or technique or methodology is not the most important variable in raising children. Maybe it's more nuanced than that. Maybe it has more to do with alignment than approach. Perhaps a parent's chief concern should be learning to listen to their own gut, to their own particular God-given constitution, to that tiny voice inside of them that nudges them one way or the other. While counselors, coaches, books, podcasts, trusted friends, our own parents (maybe), and evidence-based research are all important, the most important thing might be that quiet, unobtrusive, nebulous, in-the-background, yet unmistakable shared-DNA intuition inside of us as parents.

I didn't listen to that voice; I became tone-deaf to it. I bought into what the religious experts around me were saying, even when my gut was shouting the exact opposite. I doubted myself. I gave into guilt. I let what others thought of me enslave me. I wish I'd had more confidence. I should have silenced those booming voices and trusted the quiet one that was gurgling in my heart. I should have tuned into its frequency, noticed its unique tone, and trusted it. Because it is that God-given voice that has guided parents ever since there were parents; it is the universal parental GPS, the Spirit counselor, the particular wisdom that comes from a common gene pool.

What if I hadn't said no when Jess asked if he could go to that silly high school dance way back in the fall of 2002? What if I'd handled it more like I'd handled In-N-Out—by hearing him out, empathizing, coaching, respecting, nudging, and supporting? What if in their teen years I'd stuck closer to my gut and listened better and not been re-active; what if I'd nurtured them kindly and titrated freedoms wisely and handled pushback with grace and allowed for natural consequences to just occur whenever possible? Because I knew these young men. I knew their tendencies; I knew their hearts and their hot buttons and their fears and their insecurities and their joys and their loves. I knew when to wave the white flag and on which hill to die. I knew them like I knew myself.

Might things have turned out differently? Might Jess and Lucas not have felt the need to set the world on fire? Might they have influenced Chris differently? Maybe drugs and alcohol would have been more of a fling, like they were for me in high school, and not a way to get back at the dad they hated. I don't know. And I know the woulda-coulda-shoulda game is an endless loop and probably not worth playing. But I can't help it. In my heart I believe things would have turned out differently. And can I go out on a limb here? Can I say what I really think? I actually think they would have been very different.

19

Foxhole Faith

I was never preachy with Lucas in prison. Even though I was an ex-minister and had written the spiritually rich David letter, I'd never gotten pushy or demonstrative with him. I knew that, like most prisoners, he'd called on God many times out of panic and fear and plain old desperation. Once, when we'd talked about that kind of anguished faith, I'd called it "foxhole faith." *When you're in a foxhole, with bullets flying all around you, most of us become believers real fast.* It's as natural as a drowning man gasping for air when he breaks the surface. But I told Lucas I'd rarely seen that kind of faith last. Sure, in the moment, it feels real and produces dramatic concessions, rash bargains, and impassioned promises—but, if you think about it, they're all made under duress. When the pressure's off, they quickly fade away.

On my next visit to CRC, I used the term "foxhole faith" again and Lucas laughed, "Yeah, I remember you sayin' that."

"I know, it kinda sticks with you, doesn't it?"

"Yeah, it's funny." He mused as he stared across the patio, seeming to think out loud. "I mean, it is true, you know, to wonder if this is real, what I have in here. Is this real faith?" He hesitated and said softly, "I mean, when I get out, will I feel like I feel in here? Or are these feelings only because I'm locked up in this place?"

I shrugged. "It's not a bad question. It is a pretty surreal environment in here."

Lucas looked down at the wooden picnic table, picked at some of the thick chips of white paint, and said, "No, I get it. I do." He gazed over my shoulder. "But no, I don't think that's true for me." He shook his head and seemed agitated. "Nah, it's more than that for me; this isn't just because I'm in here. I'm not a drowning man just flailing for hope."

My eyes widened. I was intrigued by his conviction.

"Do you remember when I told you about that book I read, *Crime and Punishment*?"

I nodded.

"Yeah, well, that really affected me and made me think about rebirth and second chances, you know, the whole Lazarus thing. I was really emotional that night. I cried. And they weren't just tears of sadness. They were tears of, I don't know, joy, yeah, the joy I felt from getting a new start like that guy did." Lucas leaned forward. "Dad, that was real. That was the realest thing I've ever felt. And it's still real to me."

"Hey," I said, holding my hands up, "I'm not saying that wasn't real or that you've got foxhole faith, I'm just—"

He interrupted, "And when I started reading C.S. Lewis, it all came together. I just couldn't believe how much sense that guy made to me. I mean, I couldn't put that book down; I was reading it everywhere...like in the bathroom, at my job, in the cafeteria...even on my bunk until late at night. The way he wrote, his simple stories and analogies, brought Christianity together for me."

Lucas was breathing heavily by now, and I didn't want him to stop—I'd never seen him this animated.

But then his eyes met mine, he tilted his head, grinned, and seemed to realize he'd been on quite a rant. He leaned back, took a couple of deep breaths, and said, "No, Dad, this is going much deeper than you think."

"Hey man, I'm thrilled, don't get me wrong. It's been so cool to see you devour C.S. Lewis and Dostoevsky. I mean, incredible, like I would have never imagined! Like I wrote you when you were in Reception, there is nothing I want more in life than to see you come to faith."

He seemed to relax into what I was saying.

"But I do have this one nagging thing that just won't go away."

He squinted his eyes and said, "Wait, what?"

"Well, Lucas, there's no doubt you have the heart part of your faith down pat. I can see it so clearly and that's awesome. But I do wonder about the head part. You know, your mind, your intellect?"

"What do you mean?"

"Well, you know how the Bible says to love God with your heart and soul?"

"Yeah."

"Well, it also says to love him with your mind and strength. You know, your intellect, the left side of your brain. And for years, before prison and all, you told me you had trouble reconciling God with science and evolution. You felt that somehow, they disproved God or went against the Bible. Am I right?"

He nodded.

"I just think that you gotta confront those questions head-on. You know, maybe study evolution and the sciences and see if they disprove God like you thought they did. Dig into astronomy and physics and geology and chemistry and see if God and evolution are in fact incompatible."

He jutted out his lower jaw as if he were chewing on what I was saying.

"Because, Lucas, think about it. If you don't really go there, I mean, *really* go there, if you don't confront your doubts head-on, I'm afraid that the faith you have in here will be wishful thinking. It won't last. Your brain's gotta be a believer, too."

"Okay, so let's say you're right," he replied. "So what do I do? I mean, how am I going to do that in here? They won't even let us get online."

"Well, I'm not sure, but if you're game, let me look into it. I've got a few ideas."

That next week I did two things: one, I searched for a book on evolution we could read together, and two, I wrote Lucas another channeling letter that addressed this issue head-on. I wrote Lucas a letter about evolution and wrote it as if I were God. Yes, I know, channeling God is the height of presumption and irreverence and probably a whole host of other sins. But I was desperate; I felt I had nothing to lose. I thought if I could somehow capture God's thinking when he used a very big bang a few billion years ago to start this whole life thing, it could really set Lucas's mind afire.

Dear Lucas,

I am. That's the best way for me to put it to you. I am. I always have been. I am right now. I always will be. I am everywhere. I am everything. I just...am.

And Lucas, I also do. I'm creative. I make things out of nothing. I created you, for example. I knew you when you were two cells in your mother's womb in Toronto in 1987—two tiny cells that contained an encyclopedia of DNA that makes you you. Those two cells then replicated into four, then eight, and so on. You grew in that dark, warm cocoon for nine months while the code in your cells grew you into you—your five-foot-ten frame, your green eyes, your dark hair, and, yes, your sweaty palms.

Even your personality traits were encased in the microscopic strands of genetic code. Your tendency toward kindness for those less fortunate, your wittiness that can sometimes turn cutting, your mental sharpness, your athleticism, and your calmness under pressure. And, yes, also your stubbornness, your selfishness, and your tendency toward excess. The raw materials that made Lucas Lucas were all encapsulated in those cells at the beginning.

But what you did with those raw materials—that was up to you. I gave you and everyone else freedom to do as you chose. That was the only way I could do it—I had to allow for options. Otherwise, I would have just created another animal, another creature of instinct on this planet—and I didn't want any more of them. And yes, I was fully aware that injecting freedom into the equation enabled both good and bad. It was a huge risk.

Free will, however, made possible the single most important thing to me: love. You could choose to love me or not. And love is only love if it's freely given. I didn't want affection out of guilt or fear or intimidation or out of obedience. I wanted a healthy love, a real one, a vibrant one—one based on passion and intrigue and awe and respect and honor and holiness. Without freedom as the baseline, none of that would have been possible.

Why love? Why was that so important to me? Why would I create a universe of such absurd proportions, with trillions of stars and light years of distance, and yet care so much about the sentiments of one little person on this one little planet? Well, because that one little person has something that no creature or ocean or mountain or star or planet has: a soul. That person has a tiny, vibrating, pulsating piece of me inside of them. We share DNA, we share spirit, we share an emotional link that is way more powerful than any gravitational, electromagnetic or nuclear force in the universe.

Lucas, I know you've felt our connection at times. Like when you've gazed at the stars or squinted through a microscope or studied a flower or gawked at the mountains or peered over the ocean. You've sensed that there's something more than the physical, something beyond just you, something beyond the curtain of your consciousness. In your heart, you know that you are more than just biology; you know you're not just a creature.

Animals, as much as I love them, and as much fun as I had bringing about the giraffe and the rhinoceros, they are not you. They're driven by instinct, by hunger, by survival, and by reproduction. Those urges unconsciously pulse through their minds and they obey accordingly. Even the dog, as loyal as he is, as filled with love as he is, as unconditionally as he loves you, as faithful a partner as he is—to the last beat of his heart—he's still a dog; he's still a creature obeying his instincts. (Well, I'm sure you know that Mumford is the one exception.)

But you are different. You contemplate today, you imagine tomorrow, and you remember yesterday. You search for meaning and are drawn to art and elegance and creativity. A simple song can reduce you to tears or inspire you to love. A poem can clarify the undecipherable. A pink and orange sunset will have you reflexively reaching into your back pocket for your phone. (The panther doesn't admire a sunset—he simply prepares to hunt.) You invent and innovate. You can't help but advance technology. You serve and sacrifice. You run into burning buildings to rescue people. You fly to foreign soil to lay down your life for your country. You work in ICUs filled with contagious patients. You are the crown of my creation and are made of my stuff.

I've told you why I did it. Now let me tell you how. I could have done it a hundred different ways. I could have done it over six days, and then taken a day off, ten thousand years ago. I know, you say that's impossible because rocks on the globe are older than that. Fair enough. But come on, if I can create the universe, I can create a rock with accelerated radioactive decay that makes it appear older than it really is. That would be the least of my challenges. Or I could have made the universe almost fourteen billion years ago and let it evolve into the state you now see. Why not?

I could have compressed matter (as you know it) into an inconceivably dense pinpoint of pure energy—a singularity, if you will—and then infused it with even more energy, forcing a massive explosion, or a "Big Bang." This would give birth to the physical universe you now see. Time, space, and matter would all begin in that fraction of a second.

The explosion would expand, change, and coalesce into a seemingly ever-expanding system. As the universe cooled, energy would change into particles you call protons and neutrons, eventually forming hydrogen and helium nuclei. Matter would then combine into galaxies and, under the force of gravity, start to rotate the way you see now.

Your sun would form as a third-generation star. Your planet, initially a hot mess, would slowly cool and become hospitable for life about four billion years ago. Through a combination of solar energy, radioactive cells, water, and oxygen, life would begin at its most basic cellular level about one hundred fifty million years later. Cells would start interacting with each other so that when one organism developed a protein that was advantageous, that new capability would be quickly replicated by other organisms. The globe would become a mass commune of self-improving cells.

About four hundred million years ago, this survival of the fittest would cause plants to appear. Thirty million years after that, animals would move on the land. Then dinosaurs, whose reign ended cataclysmically with a giant meteor, would make way for humans to prosper, about sixty-five million years ago.

I know I'm throwing around millions of years as if they were dice, and it's very hard for you to grasp the spans of time I'm talking about. But if natural evolution is how I created everything, I needed enormous periods of time to do so because evolutionary improvements are so infinitesimally small most of the time.

So yes, Lucas, I could have used the process of evolution. And with the progress of scientific research in your time, many of the discoveries point in that exact direction. And I'm glad they do. Science and I aren't mutually exclusive. In fact, if you think about it, science is the study of me, my creation, and my creativity. Most scientists, especially late in their careers, end up in awe of what I've created, humbled at its complexity and simplicity and elegance. They may not call me by name, but many of them praise the idea of me.

So when did humans transition from creature to image-of-God creation? Did I interrupt natural evolution to infuse the human with a soul? Yes, I did. And I did it in a garden. That's where biology met eternity. That's where the tree of the knowledge of good and evil was plucked, and the fruit was eaten. And with that one act, you gained knowledge and wisdom and goodness and complexity and depth and joy. But with that act you also gained evil and shame and sorrow and fear and death and sweat on the brow and thorns in the hand. In the garden was birthed the possibility of love and kindness and compassion and humility and the laying down one's life for a friend. But also birthed was the ability to hate, to be cruel and heartless and arrogant, and to kill.

I knew the garden would open it all up. I knew it would change everything. And you may wonder, was it worth it? Was the good worth the evil? After seeing war and the holocaust and what humans can do to each other and to animals and to the planet, would I do it again? Lucas, I don't expect you to understand this, but, yes, I would. In fact, I'll say, absolutely yes. Because of the overwhelming, mysterious, complicated beauty of love between Creator and created, it was worth it. I would have it no other way. To me, reciprocity is priceless.

So back to that packet of DNA, which contains those four simple letters in the alphabet—A, C, G, and T—the letters that make you, you. They make the physical you, but they don't make the spiritual you. Your soul is not dictated by biology or chemistry. You, Lucas, make your soul what it will be.

We've never quite gelled, you and me. I've hoped for it, and anticipated it, but it never quite came together. We got close a couple times, though. Once when you were in a cabin one summer, way up high in the mountains, you heard the touching story of a college student finding me after suffering through years of abuse and loneliness. And you leaned into me. I felt it. You looked around that cabin as if I was hidden behind the bunkbed. You felt me tugging on your heart. But it didn't quite happen; the world got in the way. I knew there'd be other times, but I left that in your court. Yes, I tugged and gently prodded every once in a while, but when it comes to an "us," you hold all the cards.

I know you've been praying to me a lot lately. I know that prison will do that to you, and I hear a lot of prayers from there. It's as natural as breathing, and I don't begrudge anyone for it. But I don't want desperate love. I don't want people only calling on me when they're flat on their back. I want genuine love. I want healthy love.

Lucas, take your time; you have lots of it. Use this prison term to learn about me. I love your new interest in reading. Read my book. Read books about me. Maybe we never connected because you were too busy and too distracted. Maybe you thought that fourteen-billion-year evolution somehow disproved my existence. I don't know the reason, but it doesn't matter now.

Your life has changed forever. But Lucas, it's not over. You're still alive. And please, don't get lost trying to figure out why you lived and another man died. I don't mean to patronize you, but it's beyond you. Focus, instead, on living a life worth living. Wrestle meaning out of meaninglessness. Change. Grow. Be better. Make what happened a rebirth. You may drive yourself crazy trying, but try anyway.

As your Father and Creator, I hope you'll lean in again one day. And when you feel that tug on your heart, look for me, look around. Maybe it'll be in a room that looks like that cabin in the mountains, or maybe it'll be in a dorm full of grown men, in a place surrounded by razor wire. I don't care where it is, I just care that there becomes an "us."

Love, God (and Pops)

Dear Pops,

I loved that letter. To be honest, it moved me to tears, and I had to stop reading it. Okay, I know you've written me a lot of letters, and I've loved them all but I gotta tell you, even more than David, this one was my favorite. And then when you wrote about the dog and his loyalty and love, I just wept. Man, I miss my dog.

Anyway, when I read it, I was on my rack and poured through it like a maniac. When I was done, just like I did after I finished Dostoevsky, I laid it on my chest, stared at the ceiling, and thought about God in a whole new way. I mean it opened my mind and made me see him as more personal and interested and creative. And, in a way, more scientific.

Love, Lucas

The week after writing this letter, I found a book that was the scientific version of my letter. It's called *The Language of God: A Scientist Presents Evidence for Belief.* The book is an argument for rational faith, under the premise that God created humankind through an evolutionary process. How perfect is that? Francis Collins, the author, a physician-geneticist who led the Human Genome Project under President Bush and Clinton, and then directed the National Institute of Health under Obama, Trump, and Biden, had an uncanny ability to marry science and faith—without soiling either. He took readers on a stunning tour of physics, chemistry, and biology to show that all the sciences were compatible with a belief in God and the Bible.

Unlike anyone else who might tackle the subject, Collins had credibility with both the faith and the science community. And he wasn't afraid to challenge both groups. He boldly confronted believers, challenging them not to bury their heads in the sand about science and the natural world. Then he vigorously challenged the scientific community to consider the moral argument for God's existence, as well as numerous physical features of the universe that suggest an active creator instead of mere chance. He states, "I find theistic evolution to be by far the most scientifically consistent and spiritually satisfying of the alternatives. This position will not go out of style or be disproven by future scientific discoveries. It is intellectually rigorous, it provides answers to many otherwise puzzling questions, and it allows science and faith to fortify each other like two unshakable pillars, holding up a building called Truth." Later he states, "Science's domain is to explore nature. God's domain is in the spiritual world, a realm not possible to explore with the tools and language of science. It must be examined with the heart, the mind, and the soul—and the mind must find a way to embrace both realms."

This book enriched my own faith. It outlined what I had long believed in a general sense but couldn't put into words. Now I had facts and arguments and logic and science to support my intuition. Since reading this book, I have never looked at the stars or the mountains or the human body or plants in the same way—they are all more bedazzling. Hiking has become a spiritual exercise for me. Gardening is an act of symbiosis. Sitting in my Jacuzzi, which I do every night, and viewing the stars in that dark sky, is endlessly stimulating. Nova has now become my favorite TV show.

Lucas loved the book, too. Besides Dr. Collins's eloquent integration of God and science, his personal journey from atheism to faith mirrored Lucas's in a way. Both of them were captivated by the book *Mere Christianity* by C.S. Lewis. In it, CS (as we came to call him) presents a series of lectures he did for BBC radio during World War II, in which he simply, logically, cleverly, and with lively metaphors, makes as compelling a case for God as any that exists:

"When you come to knowing God, the initiative lies on His side. If He does not show Himself, nothing you can do will enable you to find Him. And, in fact, He shows much more of Himself to some people than to others—not because He has favorites, but because it is impossible for Him to show Himself to a man whose whole mind and character are in the wrong condition. Just as sunlight, though it has no favorites, cannot be reflected in a dusty mirror as clearly as in a clean one."

"If the whole universe has no meaning, we should never have found out that it has no meaning: just as, if there were no light in the universe and therefore no creatures with eyes, we should never know it was dark. Dark would be without meaning."

"A man who was merely a man and said the sort of things Jesus said would not be a great moral teacher. He would either be a lunatic—on a level with the man who says he is a poached egg—or else he would be the Devil of Hell. You must make your choice"

Absolutely no one could say it like CS. No one had his plain, vivid, jarring, folksy way, backed with as vigorous a mind as the twentieth century had produced.

My single favorite phone call from Lucas over his almost three years in prison occurred when he finished *The Language of God*. He was talking so fast I couldn't keep up with him. He said he could barely sleep at night trying to absorb the altruism argument, the implications of physical constants like the speed of light, the science used to determine a billions-of-years-old universe, and the persuasive account of natural selection as the crucial generator of the diversity and complexity of life here on earth.

I said very little on this fifteen-minute phone call. I just smiled and listened. This was not my son. He had never been much of a reader or a thinker or a man of faith. But now he was talking my ear off about things I didn't even understand, and writing me six-page letters, front and back, quoting Dumas, Vonnegut, Aurelius, Lucado, and C.S. Lewis.

I didn't know what to make of this. I had no idea where it would land or whether it was foxhole faith. Would it lead to change and a drug-free life? A productive life? To faith? I didn't know. But I've always believed that knowledge can change a man. Stimulating the mind can fire up the heart.

20

Alternating Visits

Lucas had been at CRC for over a year, and every other weekend Joyce and I would visit him together. On other weekends, Jess, Chris, or other friends would visit him as well.

On one of our patio visits, Lucas told me and Joyce that he'd had an altercation that week on the basketball court. Before he finished explaining what happened, Joyce quipped, "Did you get in trouble?"

"Wait," I said, impatiently, "let him finish telling us what happened."

He told us that one of the guys on the opposing team had been trash-talking him and throwing elbows all over the place.

Joyce interjected, "So did you get written up?"

"No, I was lucky. This guard who knows me saw the whole thing and let me off."

"So who was this guy who wanted to fight you?" I asked. "Do you know him? Have you guys had words?"

Before he could answer, Joyce slipped in quietly, "Lucas, you gotta be careful. You know if you get written up, it could add years to your sentence."

"Mom, I know that," he said curtly. "It was just, you know, this stuff happens, especially on the court, and you can't just let some guy punk you. You can't do that in here. Anyway, this guy, yeah, we've never gotten along and uh..."

Under her breath, Joyce mumbled, "Yeah, but it's not worth it."

I glared at Joyce.

She lifted both hands and said, "Wait, I...I...just can't help myself. Lucas, you finish the story, and I'll make a run to the snack bar. How about that?"

As soon as Joyce was gone, Lucas turned to me and said, "You guys do that a lot, you know, that thing you just did."

I looked down and shook my head. "I know, it's really embarrassing. Mom just gets so excited to see you, and we talk over each other, and then I interrupt, or she does, and then we snip at each other. We're like that crotchety old married couple. I know it probably makes you feel awkward."

"Yeah, it is a little uncomfortable, but I can see how it happens." He leaned back. "You know what? I have an idea. What if you guys visited on different weekends?"

I looked at him sheepishly.

"No, think about it. It would give Mom a break, you know, a few weekends off. And then when she came, I'd be all hers. We do talk about completely different things than you and I do."

"Well, I gotta admit, that does sound kinda interesting." I pondered the idea. "I mean, maybe it could work. How about I run it by your mom on our way home?"

An hour later, as we sped down the highway, I casually told Joyce what Lucas had suggested, wanting to make sure she knew it was his idea, not mine.

Joyce didn't take her eyes off the road and kept her hands at ten and two. I waited, hoping she wouldn't launch into a discourse about how I interrupted her or how I never listened to her or how I'd never listened to her one time in our thirty-five years of marriage. But without looking over at me she said, "I think it's a good idea."

I stayed quiet for a beat, expecting some follow-up about how we should do better and respect each other and not talk over each other. But she said nothing.

"Sooo, you're fine with it, it's not a problem...like with us or anything?"

"Nope, it sounds good to me," she said, without even a hint of self-pity.

I leaned back in my seat, absorbing what alternating visits might look like, and said, "Okay, well, since you do the schedule, would you mind just putting me on the weekend that you want me to go. How's that sound?"

"Yup, we'll do it," she said lightheartedly.

And that was that. We discussed it no further. Over the next few days, I thought about our interaction and was both relieved and embarrassed. Relieved because it did simplify our visits and actually seemed like a good idea. But I was also a little embarrassed that we'd just so quickly accepted separation instead of working through a problem. It felt almost like a defeat, like we couldn't get along, so instead of talking about it, we just decided to sleep in different bedrooms. I mean, could we not just solve this? Could we not just bite our tongues for a couple hours for the sake of our incarcerated son? Couldn't we behave ourselves so our son could be around some normal human beings for a change?

This pattern, doing stuff separately, had become a real part of our marriage. Joyce and I didn't play any sports together, we would never go to the gym together, and we didn't enjoy shopping together like many of the couples we knew. If we went to church, at least at that time, it was often different churches—only because we felt like we needed different things. Joyce had an active social life, but I'd become increasingly solitary, preferring to hike with Mumford and spend days and days in the mountains.

After this visit with Lucas, I had the fleeting thought that maybe we were drifting from each other in an unhealthy way. We had talked about it for years and viewed our independence as a strength, not a weakness. Joyce just didn't want me shopping with her. The thought of me peering over her shoulder in a Vons grocery store, or really any store, gave her the heebie jeebies. She loved that time alone. And I loved my mountain time alone. We had come to believe that we just weren't that couple that finishes each other's sentences and wants to do everything together.

But we know that autonomy also has its risks. You can drift from your partner and suddenly find yourself with someone you don't even know, living a life very different from your own. We've seen that happen to other couples, and we've talked about making sure it doesn't happen with us. But importantly, we are joined at the hip on the big things. That lunch thing—it's still true. You know, that one-person-in-the-world thing—yeah, it's still Joyce. Our spiritual migration, as independent and circuitous as it was over those fifteen years of family challenges, has landed us in the same place. If it hadn't, if either of us had let our bitterness drive us from God, I think we could be in some serious trouble. Oh, and the biggie: we both love us some *Grey's Anatomy*. Yes, we are currently binging all eighteen seasons for the second time through.

It turned out the solo visits with Lucas were a boon. He and I had the best walk-and-talks we'd ever had, pacing the fence, firmly establishing that path in the crabgrass. They were talks we would have never had if someone else had been with us. Joyce, too, loved her visits alone with him.

For our thirty-ninth anniversary, I gave Joyce an envelope with four Benjamins in it—four one-hundred-dollar bills. Joyce is a gift giver, and I've learned that the ultimate gift for such a person is cash (yes, I know, the height of romance). On the actual bills, I noticed there were passages from the Declaration of Independence, a document that proclaims the virtues of solidarity and autonomy. I laughed at the irony of giving her bills with that text on them. Then I wrote her a poem and integrated some of the themes from that document. As I finished, I thought, *This is so us. I'm quoting a document that's all about independence— on our anniversary!* I think Ben would've chuckled.

21

Letter to the Widow

On the second anniversary of the accident, Lucas wrote the widow.

He was in a brand-new place intellectually and emotionally, and for the first time, he could write a thoughtful, heartfelt—but not over-the-top—letter. Months before the May 25 date, he wrote a first draft and slept on it for a week. Then we talked about it over the phone. He rewrote it and mailed me a copy, asking for my input. He worked on it some more and then talked it over with his counselor and college professor. Then he came up with a final draft.

It wasn't the first time he'd written her and apologized. His first had been in open court on the day of his sentencing—basically, a tear-filled outburst. His second apology had been a letter on the *first* anniversary of the accident. In it, he spilled out unprocessed emotions, and it sent him into a tailspin of depression that lasted for several weeks. He told me that as he wrote, he was haunted by her face from that day in the courtroom. He couldn't get over her sadness and innocence.

But this letter was different. It struck the right tone. He told her up front that he would fail in trying to express all the emotions bottled up inside of him, but he must try. He must try for her sake—and his. He wanted to tell her that he'd changed his life and recovered and rehabilitated himself and become a different man. He wanted to thank her for being gracious and not unloading on him on the day of sentencing. He wanted to apologize once again for fleeing the scene like a coward. He wanted to tell her his belief that true redemption happened when guilt led a man to do good. He wanted to tell her that he would live a good life so that Rod's death would not be in vain. And ultimately, he had to tell her again, for the umpteenth time, that he was sorry. What happened on that road haunted him every day of his life.

He told me all the reading, writing, and studying he'd been doing had refreshed his mind and given him new things to say along with new conviction to say them. He knew she probably didn't care one whit about how much he had changed his life—and she might even resent him for telling her about it—but he had to tell her. He had to let her know.

Ironically, although he'd written the letter for her, it changed his life. After he mailed it, I could swear he stood taller, his eyes were sharper, and the tears—which for two years had snuck out from behind his eyes any time I brought up the accident—disappeared. He spoke more confidently and wrote more clearly as he settled into new terms with an old wound. He said it helped him find a semblance, although only a semblance, of peace. He confided in me that he wished the same for the widow.

Lucas told me that most inmates in the yard took pride in their crime. They'd brag about what they'd done, or blame the victim, or blame the system. It was always someone else's fault. It was so consistent among inmates that it turned him off, and actually made him lean in even more to owning his own crime.

Obviously, I would never share his letter to the widow with anyone—it's for her eyes only—but I did write to Lucas after he mailed it.

Dear Lucas,

Son, I gotta tell you, I'm proud of you for that letter you wrote to Valerie. You did the most difficult thing a man can do—you admitted the truth, in all its ugliness, and apologized for what you did. And you did it with great specificity and humility and realness. You can't do any more than that.

I'm glad you took months to craft it. I'm glad you cycled through that roller coaster of emotion and found some real things to say. I think you succeeded at the nearly impossible because you're in a new place mentally, spiritually, and emotionally. When you told me your plan—to write her on the anniversary—I thought the timing was perfect. You seemed ready and able, for the first time, to capture it all without bleeding all over the page.

You acknowledged the utter inadequacy of words—but wrote them anyway. All five pages. For her. And for you.

You owned your mistake fully. No equivocation. No excuses.

You shared how you've changed and will never forget Rod. Or her.

You apologized for your cowardice when you fled the scene. I'm so glad you put that in there, too. I know you said it at the sentencing, but who knows what she heard that day.

I know it pains you that you will never know how she feels about what you wrote her. It pains me, too. But in the end, you know, it really doesn't matter. You've done what you can do. And, most importantly, to her, and to God, and to your own self, you've made sure the accident and your incarceration have not all been in vain.

And for that, son, I'm proud of you. I really am.

Love, Pops

Years later, as I read this letter, I wondered if pride was the right emotion to express. To be honest, it feels a little off to me now and almost makes me squirm. Sure, I was proud of Lucas, proud he'd come back from rock bottom and completely transformed himself. I was proud that he'd poured out his heart to the woman whose husband he killed, that he'd owned his actions, every one of them, without one hedge. Sure, there was plenty to be proud of.

But to bring that word back into our relationship scared me. It made me feel vulnerable, like I might be setting myself up for disappointment again. I know this is probably just a bad case of parental PTSD, but that's how it hit me.

Maybe I'm just scared Lucas will relapse. Or maybe I don't want to put the pressure of my expectations on him. Maybe I don't want to link our relationship to his actions in a way that's not healthy for him or for me. As he moves on from the accident, his addiction, and his incarceration, I want to be happy for him, delighted when things go his way, and yes, filled with parental satisfaction when he matures. I just don't want to call it pride.

Lucas knows my hopes for him. We have bonded like few men do. But I don't want him to feel the burden of my pride. He may slip up. Or he may never abuse substances again. He may become an amazing husband and father and man. He may become a lover of God. He may share his renaissance with thousands, or just with a handful of friends. I don't know what he'll do or what kind of man he'll become. I just don't want my pride, or lack of it, to drive him one way or the other. I want to get out of the way and allow him to become the man he wants to become, while cheering him from the sidelines.

Maybe that's all just another word for pride.

22

Two Men

Lucas wrote me this letter on my fifty-ninth birthday, four months before his release from prison.

Dear Pops,

One man lies in bed, quiet, restless, gazing out the steel-barred window to the gray sky. The early dawn silence is subtle and eerie. It's always like this; every morning's the same.

His mind is already reeling. He hates that it always does—he wishes he could just turn it off. He sits up and pushes the bed sheets off—it was another sleepless night. He yawns and stretches out his arms and legs and then pulls his clothes from his laundry line. He can feel he is getting older—his knees and back ache. He rolls up the tattered sleep mat and positions it at the end of his bunk along with his folded sheets. He scooches off the squeaking metal rack and hears the sound of feet shuffling outside his door as men march to the bathroom to start their morning routine.

Another man also stirs, not to an alarm or to the sound of shuffling feet, but to an inner urge, to a drive that pushes him. His house is silent, and his bed creaks when he gets up. He glances at the clock on the nightstand, and it reads 5:09 a.m. The house is chilly, and a breeze flows through a partly opened window. He walks quietly on the soft, carpeted floor so as to not wake his wife. He shuts the bedroom door, takes in a deep breath, and relishes the thought that the world is still asleep.

He takes the five steps to his office and starts typing on his computer, reminiscent of a mad scientist, but with no lab coat or chemicals. He's hunched, pressing keys, typing, typing, typing, seated in a high-back leather chair, using a sleek laptop set upon a long wooden desk. He whispers words, ideas, and thoughts to himself, his eyes pinned to the monitor, the words spilling out of a well he didn't even know existed. This man is a writer. He always has been, although never officially. He's a simple man, one who thinks clearly, one who sees what others don't, one who believes decisively and lives uniquely. Now his office has become his sanctuary, his creative space, and a place to process life with a son in prison.

The son opens his locker, ladles a tablespoon of instant coffee into a cup, and joins the other men for the monotonous march to the bathroom, each of them numb and indifferent to the coming day. He waits his turn for hot water from the sink and thinks about how he is always waiting for something. There are so many men here. They are everywhere, all the time. They wander, they form lines, they move aimlessly, all with nothing to do but hurry up and wait. He doesn't want to become one of them. He resists the urge every day. But it pulls on him, it drags at him, it's a constant fight not to become one of them.

He returns to his room with a hot cup of coffee. For a moment, he sits there, staring down at the chipped, rusted metal rack that is his bed. His mind is blank, his thoughts are empty. He detaches from his past and present existence; they are dead to him. Suddenly a fresh scent of pine from the open window jolts him back to where he is. He hates being yanked back to the present.

The father's dog lies at his feet, in a trance from the sound of rhythmic keyboard clicks. The dog's eyes are eager and alert, noticing each movement or chair creak, eager for the signal that it's time to hit the trail. Light is now hitting the mountains outside the father's large office window, turning the grays to pink. He pushes back his chair, puts on a long-sleeve T-shirt and a light Patagonia jacket, and heads to the garage to put on his hiking shoes. Man and dog head out the back garage door and ascend a hill that forms an amphitheater around the back of his house. He has spent hours on that hill, terracing it and planting an orchard. The ground is soft with morning dew, and a flock of quail noisily take flight as man and dog pass a giant oak tree he planted twenty-five years ago.

After climbing the hill for fifteen minutes, he stops to survey the view at the summit. It reminds him of what brings him joy: to ascend mountains and look at what lies below. He lives for these simple moments at sunrise, the moments that remind him of his Creator, the moments he witnesses the detail and harmony and beauty of nature. He thanks God and then looks down at his dog. This little creature has been everywhere with him. He is, in a way, his best friend.

The son puts on his blue shirt and pants, laces up his brown boots, and gets ready for work. He reads two chapters from Romans and says a silent prayer. He grabs his paperwork, Stephen King's On Writing book, and his most important possession, his black-and-white checkered composition notebook. He walks to his friend's cell and knocks.

"Ready?" he asks. "Let's go."

They walk into the now rising sun, the yellow rays hitting the hardened ground.

His friend jokes, "You ready to suck this day's dick?"

He laughs. "I guess we don't really have a choice."

This is how they talk in this place. The baseness of prison life bringing out the baseness of humor. They want to get a reaction, a laugh, anything to show a sign of life. They reach the front gate, which is connected to a twenty-foot-high barbed-wire fence that borders the entire yard, and they wait. They are always waiting.

Then they hear, "Yard down! Yard down! Get the fuck down!"

Everyone drops to the ground.

He hugs the dirt, but he's not worried. This has happened a hundred times before—probably a fight or some medical issue. As he waits for the alarm to be called off, he props himself up on his elbows and looks beyond the gate. The prison is on a hill overlooking a sleepy neighborhood down below. He looks at the houses, each with a small backyard, cars and RVs parked out front, and the large shade trees lining the street. He dreams of the lives they must be living down there—barbecues on Sunday, watching football, laughing, and girls everywhere. It's a distant memory, a previous life, so close to him he can taste it.

His friend asks, "What do you think about when you look out there?"

He laughs. "Shit, all sorts of shit."

The father hikes down from the summit and drops into a park lined with bushes and oaks and pines. He is the only one there. The park has a basketball court, a playground with swings, and a wide couple acres of grass between the two. His dog takes off, chasing rabbits and fetching frisbees, just like his first dog did many years before. He used to bring his sons here to play. They would swing, play soccer, and when they got older, spend all their time on the basketball court. It was a simpler time back then.

He and his dog hike back home, and he pauses before he descends the hill to his house. Memories flash. He remembers that this hilltop is where he buried his first dog, and he will do the same with this one. He remembers that this hilltop is where his oldest son proposed to his fiancée, now wife. He thinks of his grandson and the new granddaughter he's always wanted. He remembers that his middle son, the one who is now in prison, is the one who cleared all the bushes off this hill so he could plant trees. He remembers, on this mountain, reading words to his wife on their thirty-fifth anniversary. Sweat drips down his forehead, and he wipes it with the back of his hand, tasting salt in his mouth. He looks to the sky and says a silent prayer of thanks and a prayer for his son in prison. The sun shines brightly behind his back now. He lets out a high-pitched "hup" for his dog, and they trudge down the hill together.

The son sits in a metal chair in a long hallway reminiscent of a hospital corridor, with pale tile floors and chipped white walls. He dials a number, it rings twice, the operator says to press five to process the charges. He waits to be connected.

"Kenny G," he says cheerfully.

"Lucas James, what's up, my man?"

"Nothin', just wanted to see what you're up to."

"Oh, we're just out to dinner."

The father doesn't like to share about the amazing restaurants he eats at. It's just too painful for his son, whose cafeteria tray sees only grays and browns. But his son doesn't mind. In fact, he takes pleasure in hearing about the salmon belly, the filet mignon, and the baby back ribs.

"So where are you guys eating for your birthday?"

"Oh, we're at Love Sushi. You know me."

Of course, *he thinks*, that man loves him some sushi. *He's heard all about that place and how it was "hog heaven" and how he sang Hallelujah right there in the restaurant while his wife shrunk down in her seat out of embarrassment. But this man doesn't care what others think. He's gonna live life as he chooses, on his own terms, in his own unique way.*

"Well, happy birthday, old man. You deserve it."

"Thanks, I really wish you were here."

"Me too," he says. "This will be the last one I will miss."

"I sure hope so."

When he hangs up the phone, he grabs his blue shirt and ID from his rack and heads out to the night yard. He spins a lap around the track. The sun is setting, and the sky is orange and yellow. He stops at the fence overlooking the neighborhoods below and enjoys the best thing about this prison: this view. His hands clench the metal links, and his eyes go dull looking over the city below.

"Hey, dude! Hands off the fence!" *a guard yells.*

"Shit," *he says under his breath, and he walks off, irritated. He walks back to his building, down the long hallway that leads to his room. TVs are blaring, men are laughing, a guard is yelling, but he hears nothing.*

It is what it is, he says to himself. Everything is strangely as it should be. This is his new normal, and he's not scared by it, but he knows he should be.

He jumps up onto his rack and lies on the cold, hard metal. He studies the ceiling, the details of the cracks, the monotony of the white, and there is a calmness in his chest. He feels like he's back home. Now he's at peace.

Love, Lucas

23

Reality LA

Almost everyone claims some sort of PTSD these days. So much so that it seems to have lost its oomph. But I'm still going to claim it. Not uppercase PTSD—you know, the kind diagnosed by a doctor that might settle in after a sexual assault, warfare, or a traffic accident. I'm going to claim the lowercase version—the kind that is trauma and stress, and, at least to me, has become a disorder.

Mine was spiritual PTSD. It was the stress I felt after my traumatic breakup with a church of thirty years, my traumatic family implosion, my traumatic crisis of faith, and my traumatic experience with Lucas. When the accident happened, I knew I needed help. I was spiritually numb. I needed something, some sort of jump start or bridge or intervention.

Writing the David letter, several months after the accident, helped. It broke me out of my Bible sabbatical, true, but it was only so much. I needed more.

At the time, through podcasts and the news, I was hearing a lot about people finding great success at overcoming trauma by using psychedelics. And the idea made sense to me. You're stuck, you see the world one way, you can't break out of your own endless loop, and then bam, you take psilocybin, you see the world differently, your brain skips out of the old loop, forms a new path, and now you have a new channel of thinking. I know I'm not only oversimplifying it, but probably misstating it, too, but that's essentially what I gleaned from all the things I heard and read. It made me wonder if I needed something like that for my spiritual life. My loops were well worn, and I was having trouble getting out of the ruts.

Then I showed up at this place in Hollywood. No, not what you think...it was a church. But a very different kind of church. Not in its doctrine but in its candescence. The lights were low when I walked into the large high school auditorium where the services of Reality LA were held. Then the lights were dimmed even more when the singing started—way down, almost to complete darkness except for rope lights on the aisles and illumination from the large screens onto which the lyrics were cast. Even the band was in the dark, each of the members with a small light atop their music stand.

At first, I was taken aback, I couldn't even see my neighbor. But soon I relaxed; soon I settled into the vibe. I started to see the value of the darkness. In fact, I started to love it. It made me invisible; it enabled me to relax into the song and what the song was sucking out of me and the emotions that were bubbling up within me. In darkness, I could let go, I could feel what I was feeling and actually connect with the internal me, the real me, because no one, not one soul, could see me.

During the songs, I cried like I never had in church, often dropping my head, tears streaming down my face, throat too swollen to sing any more, hunched over, leaning on the chair in front of me, wondering if I would feel a hand on my shoulder and hear the words, "Hey man, are you okay?" *I'm not okay,* I would have said, *I'm really not. I'm messed up. I don't know what I believe anymore. I don't know about God. I don't know anything about anything anymore.*

But I was *getting* okay. This weekly catharsis in the dark was moving something inside of me; it was helping me process my disappointment and helping me come to terms with God. I saw I wasn't so far from him; he was right there. And weirdly, the more tears I shed, the better I felt.

Was this my version of a psychedelic trip? Was the music lifting me out of my normal groove and elevating me and moving me and helping me to see things differently? Was the darkness enabling me to lose myself and push aside my ego so I would be open to newness? I don't exactly know. But that's kind of how it felt to me. It was that transformative. It felt very similar to how I'd heard others describe their psychedelic experience.

While I was attending Reality LA, I would tell Lucas about it on the phone or when I saw him at CRC. But it wasn't until near the end of his time there that I told him of my out-of-body experiences.

Dear Lucas,

We've talked about that church I found in Hollywood—you know, the one with that great name: Reality LA (ugh, just too LA). Well, I wanted to give you an update.

I finally figured out why I love the music so much: it's a cross between Mumford & Sons and Hillsong UNITED, two of my favorite bands. They have all the instruments of a rock band, but also a cello, a fiddle, a stand-up bass, and even an old-school squeeze-box. Yeah, as soon as I saw the squeeze-box (which is kinda like an accordion), I knew I'd like this place. They could swell and temper a song with the precision of a fine chef leading your palette through an exquisite five-course dinner. They'd build the song, accentuate the lyrics, bring it down at exactly the right time, and my tears would flow. A minute later, they'd swell it and I'd be ready to shoot my hands in the air with joy.

Your mom came with me at first, but I think it was a little much for her, so she opted for a more conventional service closer to home. The more I attended, though, the more I gave myself over to the experience. I realized I needed the music; I needed the darkness. I needed the music in the darkness. It ministered to my soul and compelled me to get real with myself. It quieted my ego and my self-consciousness and my need to appear like a normal person. Here I could just let go and let the tears flow and embrace a simple faith. I could admit I didn't have many answers and that I was discouraged beyond words. This form of worship wasn't about solutions or answers or epiphanies. It was about getting in touch with my feelings. And as cliché and corny as that sounds, I needed help processing all the weight I had been carrying for a long time.

It was wild to watch happen. One Sunday, I tried to step outside myself and observe what was going on during the service. That day I felt normal, not emotional in any way. The music started with a repeating bass riff and I settled into the rhythm. A cellist pulled her bow across the thick strings and the entire room vibrated with a glorious shake. I felt my throat tighten as her instrument seemed to reach into my heart and tug on it. Then a bass drum sounded and stopped. Then beat, then rested, starting a slow, methodical dirge that pulled me along into the song. I'm theirs, I thought, I'm ready to go wherever they lead. There is just something about that low register, especially the cello, delivered discreetly and elegantly, that can tighten my throat and make me well up. Once the lyrics were displayed and the band started to swell the song and tears spilled from my eyes, my little outside-myself observation vanished into the darkness.

I remember one time, after something challenging happened to you in jail, or maybe it was after I wrote that stupid Dexter letter, I was feeling especially insecure and emotional. I was seated close to the stage and the bright lyrics on the screen shone on me like a spotlight. In my melancholy, I felt like all my defeats and disappointments and dismays were piled up in front of me, in plain sight of everyone. In that discouraged frame of mind, some words appeared on the screen that sparked something inside of me. I suddenly thought, I believe those words, I believe what they say. And instantly, I went from depressed to someone desperately clinging to those words. To be honest, I don't remember the lyric exactly, but it must have been an affirmation I could agree with, something like: "I am who you say I am," or, "God is my refuge in times of trouble." Something like that. And that simple affirmation, or as I call it, that simple "glomming onto," lifted me out of myself and focused me on a truth that felt truer than my feelings. I know it may sound insignificant—especially since I can't remember the exact lyric—but as I look back on it now, a couple years later, that Sunday marked a turning point for me. From that day on my spiritual countenance and confidence started to improve, and I've been getting stronger since then.

The preaching at this place, on the other hand, is kinda the opposite. Not that the minister wasn't fine—he was. And not that he didn't teach well—he did. But it was just hard to hear preaching of any type. It hit me as...well, preachy, and overly ordered and packaged and tied up in a nice, neat bow. At first, I tried to mentally relax and take it in with a Buddha-like calm, but I just couldn't. Then I rebuked myself for my arrogance and insolence, but that didn't work either. I felt like Jim Carrey in Liar Liar, when he couldn't do anything to force himself to lie.

So, as embarrassing as this is to admit, I decided to stop fighting nature. At the point in the service when the preacher started walking onto the stage, I would inconspicuously duck out of my aisle seat and hurry to my car in the parking garage. I'd set my iPhone alarm for forty minutes and blissfully settle into peaceful reading or writing. Then when the piano riff started on my phone, I'd beeline it to my seat and enjoy another half hour of musical transcendence.

The fellowship has also proved difficult for me. Not that the people aren't nice—they are. And I love that there are many enthusiastic young people from the nearby campuses. But it's hard for me to put myself out there and glad-hand when I'm feeling so vulnerable and exposed and kinda jaded. It's like I don't want to infect them with my cynicism.

Lucas, I feel like my whole spiritual life has been upended. And now I'm just trying to figure out what I believe. I don't want what I used to have—that I know. But I also don't want to be just spiritual, you know, spiritual but not Christian. No, I want to be a Christian. I want to hold close to the Bible. I just don't want to be so judgy and so sure of myself, thinking that I'm the only one who's right and everyone else is wrong. I don't want to be so tedious and nitpicky with the Bible, straining a gnat while swallowing a camel, as Jesus so vividly put it. I want to make the big stuff big and small stuff small. I'm not sure what this all translates into, but I'll let you know when I get there.

Something happened recently that kind of captures my spiritual life these days. I camped in the Eastern Sierra mountains, at about ten thousand feet, the weekend right before the snows hit (I got lucky). I got up before sunrise to hike west, straight into the mountains. After an hour, the sun peeked over the mountains behind me and transformed the gray granite cliffs in front of me into an almost translucent pastel pink, an alpenglow. I marveled at them and gazed just above, into the ribbon of gray-blue sky. The sun then splashed on the thousand-year-old foxtail pine trees that dotted the trail, making them look like lava lamps with their gnarled, curvy, cinnamon and blond rustic trunks. As I walked, the sun's rays began warming the fields of desert chaparral around me, so that wispy clouds wafted over the shrubs and scented the air a pungent, earthy sage.

All my senses collided, and I felt a welling up inside of me. Suddenly I stopped, doubled over my hiking poles, and broke down into tears—like really broke down. Initially I was shocked at how overwhelmed I got, but as the tears formed craters in the dust of the trail, I relaxed into my reaction and just let myself go, making my own little muddy spot in the dirt. After a few minutes, I collected myself and looked around to see if anyone else had witnessed my little outburst. Whew, it was only Mumford.

As I've thought about that little trail explosion, I don't believe it was just a me-being-overwhelmed-by-nature moment—that's happened before. This was different. This one felt Spiritual—capital 'S' spiritual. It was a God moment. Because it wasn't just my surroundings that overwhelmed me, it was the story behind them that really moved me. It wasn't just the art, but the artist himself. It was like I could see in the granite and the ancient trees and the chaparral a creative force with an artistic touch. In the clinging-to-life foxtail pines, I sensed a creator of resilience and stubbornness and doggedness. In the scent from the chaparral, I sensed an artist fascinated with subtlety and contrast.

Here I was, basking in this little serene alpine spot, the earth having heaved these cliffs up from its molten core millions of years ago. I stood in its perfect aftermath, the air on this morning eerily still, the temperature chilly, the ground fertile, the alpine plants thriving, the mountain creatures scampering about, the gnarly pines standing like proud witnesses to all this alchemy. Then I could see above the cliffs, a space beyond the sky, a haunting darkness, one that was bitterly cold and utterly lifeless, all matter expanding away from itself, as it had done for almost fourteen billion years, making this a universe of ridiculous proportions and me a speck of ridiculous insignificance. How unlikely was my pinpoint of consciousness in all this vastness? Who was I? How lucky was I to be here at this very moment in geological history? And to think that I had an "in" with the artist who conceived it. How audacious was that? How presumptuous. But in that moment, I didn't care about audacity or probability or insignificance; I cared about faith and euphoria and God and significance and the naïve belief that I was something in this everything.

This, it turned out, was one of the greatest spiritual moments of my life. And it lingers with me to this day.

Now Lucas, I can just hear you say, "Yo, Pops, that's amazing. You're crazy. Thanks for sharing. But, man, that's a lot...that's a lotta tears...are you okay?"

Well, that's a funny question, because that's what I thought I'd be asked at Reality LA when someone saw me falling apart during the song service. So let me tell you what I envisioned telling them—or at least what I would tell them now. "No, I'm not okay; I'm a mess. But I do know a couple things: I believe in God; I believe he created this universe; I believe I'm something in this vast cosmos; I believe I have a soul and that I was made in his image and that one day, in some form, in some realm, we will meet, and God and I will connect, and there will be a celebration. So let me change my answer: Yes, I'm okay. I may not be settled, and I may not look like what you think a Christian should look like. But for today, I'm okay."

And Lucas, now that I'm on a roll, let me go on. I do think it's pretty cool that I can trust-fall into music and let it swallow me whole. I think it's pretty cool that at the mere mention of the lyrics "I am who you say I am," my throat tightens and tears fill my eyes. I think it's pretty cool that I can break down on a trail in the theater of God's creation. And yes, I do cry a lot these days. I just do. The tears are just always there, close to the surface, ready to show themselves. But what am I supposed to do? I'd rather feel than not feel.

This is just the new me. This is the me who has been humbled by life, humbled by what happened to you, humbled by the mayhem that descended on our family, humbled by the scope of this universe, and humbled by the grace I've found in it. I'm a man who has seen the bottom, stared into the darkness, shivered at its emptiness, and almost slipped into it. Lucas, I almost slipped. But I didn't. I didn't lose my footing. I hung on and didn't let go and didn't curse God. I'm not going to pretend it was elegant or will make the cover of a Hallmark card. But when I think about how close I came, my throat tightens and—well, of course— my eyes fill with hot, salty tears.

I'll be the first to admit that what I have now with God is not complete. Nature is not my new religion. The universe is not my new God. Both are magnificent, but they care not one whit about me.

I'm not really sure what my new spiritual life will look like, but I know it will be simpler and less formalized and more visceral—and it will include hikes like the one I took that day.

Love, Pops

24

Letterhead

On Friday, December 14, 2018, I was working in my garden when Lucas called. "Guess what I have in my hands?" he asked. "I have no idea."

"It's a letter from the California Department of Corrections. And it has a date on it. Dad, it has a date on it!"

My stomach fluttered. "Ahhh, tell me."

Lucas's voice cracked, and he whispered, "February 12, 2019." Then there was silence. I waited. More silence. Then he haltingly said, "Sixty days from...now."

Then the line went silent again, and I knew why. This wasn't a dropped call. No inmate had interrupted him. This was silence born from a throat too swollen to talk. I'd heard that silence a dozen times over the previous three years when life had knocked the wind out of Lucas. So I just waited. I moved under the shade of my gazebo, held the phone to my ear, and waited for the silence to break. He had longed for this letter. He had worked hard to rehabilitate himself. And seeing that date, on Department of Corrections letterhead, made it real.

Finally, he whispered, "I'm just...so humbled, Dad, so grateful."

"Son, I'm so happy for you."

"I just can't believe it. I'm gonna be free in sixty days. I'm so lucky, cuz some of the guys in here—Dad, it's years, they have years...and I'm coming home."

Lucas and I talked about how things could have been so much worse. He could have so easily had seven more years. As our fifteen-minute call wound down, I asked him what he wanted for his first meal when he got home, hoping it would be sushi.

Immediately, he blurted out, "Mom's spaghetti, garlic rolls, and fresh veggies."

After getting over my disappointment, I wrote him this letter.

Dear Lucas,

Writing you changed me.

It started, really, out of desperation. We needed a way in, and letters became our last resort. At first, I sucked, with that wretched Dexter letter—thank God you still haven't read it. But hey, I got better. And then you joined in the game.

At the beginning, writing felt so old school, so stilted, so slow, so one-sided. But then I realized how difficult face-to-face was for you. With so much dark water under the bridge, so much history, so many confrontations, disagreements, and disappointments, our togetherness created an electrical charge. We needed something to absorb that current, and I think letters became that lightning rod for us.

I remember experiencing that same electrical charge with my dad. Even though I was in my late fifties and we were generally comfortable with each other, there was still something in the air between us. Oddly, the moment I realized it was when he was lying on his bed after his heart attack. He'd been cleaned up, his head was propped up, his eyes were open, and I sat down on his bed next to him. I leaned over so I could gaze directly into his eyes, and it felt like he was staring right back at me. They were the exact same eyes I'd seen all those years, but now they were just flat, just organs, with nothing behind them, no electricity, no energy, no judgment, no joy. Nothing.

A few days later, as I was thinking about that moment, I thought about how you must feel with me. You weren't in your fifties; you weren't comfortable in your skin; your life hadn't turned out as you'd hoped. Now I see that there was no way you could just blink that away when we were together. Even if I tried to make it nonintimidating—which I did—I think that as long as you were in prison, wearing blue garb, me just being your dad would distort the energy field between us. Maybe that's why letter writing became such a refuge for both of us.

It also surfaced something I didn't expect: it allowed us to say things to each other we never would have—not in a million years. Words on paper, without anyone in the room as you write them, just allow for that. Many times, I was overcome by tears while writing you—I'd stare out my window, wondering what you were doing at that moment, wondering what you were feeling, and I would write things I would've never said out loud.

About a year ago, I was cleaning out my dad's house after we sold it. In his large walk-in bedroom closet, on the top shelf, way in the back, I found a large, clear, plastic container, and pulled it down. In it were hundreds of letters he'd written to my mom while he was in Vietnam over his three tours of duty. The stack must have been six inches thick and the container two feet by two feet. I sat down to read them, and heard the words of a lonely, homesick man who loved his wife and his four kids. He was so expressive to us, writing things like, "Ken, let me compliment you on your penmanship and your work at school. Keep it up. I'm so proud of you. (Penmanship? Yeah, I guess that was a thing back then.) Your dad is still flying helicopters over here in search of Charlie. (Charlie was a stand-in for the Vietcong.) So, my young man, I want you to know I'm proud of you, and how you've stepped up and become the man of the house while I'm over here. I'm so glad you are taking care of Mom and your sisters and brother. I say a prayer for you each day that you'll grow up to be a fine gentleman. I know you will."

To my mom he wrote, "I was looking through the latest issue of National Geographic, *with several pages on Vienna, the city of songs. The pictures brought me back to the most wonderful, memorable time of my life, when I met my dear sweet wife-to-be at a kiosk on those streets. You changed my life, and I will never be the same. I'll never be able to tell you how much I appreciate what you are doing while I'm over here. You are doing wonderful work with the children. Keep it up, my dear, I love you so much." (He also wrote some not-so-subtle things about how much he missed "being with" his wife, haha. But hey, he was a man at war.)*

My mom held onto that box of letters for over fifty years, from Colorado to California to Germany to Turkey and then to their final resting place on the top shelf of a bedroom closet in Arizona. She clung to those words from her husband; they were a thing; they were tangible expressions of love; they were pen scratches on onion skin stationery, folded into ultralight airmail envelopes, bordered with short red and blue diagonal stripes. They were snapshots of a moment in time, an emotion felt in a distant land, recorded forever. The breath of words fade. The memory of a glance is forgotten. The vibration of the inner eardrum stops. But words on paper—they remain.

In my helpless, hopeless, weak-kneed sort of way, I hoped that one day you would get a box for my letters.

But I was also sobered by reading my dad's words. They weren't like him. I didn't recognize that dad. That optimistic, magnanimous, proud-of-you father was not one I saw very often. The dad I knew struggled to be positive; he became petty as he got older, and he never expressed pride in us. Even after I coauthored a good-selling business book—something I thought he would beam over—he never complimented me even once.

Lucas, I don't want you to be able to say the same thing about me. I don't want my letter-writing self to be the best version of me. I know I'm just starting to figure out Dad 2.0, and I'm not sure what he's going to look like, but I can tell you this: he'll be better and warmer and more expressive and less judgy and less intense.

I also hope you'll get a box for my letters. And when you stumble upon them one day, maybe when you're cleaning out the space above your garage, having stayed home from your construction job because of rain, and you reread them, maybe with a lump in your throat, I hope you're not surprised at the voice you hear. I hope you recognize him. I hope I live up to the letter-writing dad.

Because writing you, son, changed me.

Love, Pops

25

Cool Hand Luke

*D*ear Lucas,

It's almost over! After three long years, you're gonna be home. I can't wait to see you, but I gotta admit, I'm a bit nervous. I know that's weird, but I am. I think it's because so much has happened between us and having you out here in the real world will take some getting used to. I can only imagine how you must feel about it.

I think I'll make this my last letter to you.

About ten months after the accident, you wrote to me,

Pops, some days I barely make it in here, I mean it's totally depressing, and I struggle to pull myself out of bed. I hear all the noise around me and just want to pull the covers over my head.

Then, other days, it's the opposite. I'm filled with hope, I have faith, I can see a future. It's weird and it's hard to explain the mindset it takes to survive in here."

Hey, do you remember the movie Cool Hand Luke? Remember Luke's attitude when he was in prison, how he always had some slick, carefree reply to insults from other prisoners? Or how he wasn't bothered about being in that sweatshop? Well, that's kinda the attitude I've taken to stay sane in here. I think about it a lot: I just gotta be Cool Hand Luke and not let things get to me.

And Pops, is it not ironic that Cool Hand Luke was our movie? And then I ended up in prison just like him! How crazy is that?

Well, yeah, I agree, it's nothing short of ironic, and it's crazy. And yes, I can see how Cool Hand Luke's nothing-to-lose vibe has helped you survive.

There's a great scene in the movie I wanted to remind you of. A bunch of prisoners are hanging out playing poker. Each player gets a card in his hand and then two are flipped up in front of him. Immediately, several players fold and only Luke (Paul Newman) and another prisoner named Koko are left. Even though Koko has a pair of sevens showing and Luke has nothing, Luke raises him a dollar each time a card is dealt up. Once four cards are showing, Luke has a K-4-3 and 9 in front of him, or as the dealer shouts, "Nothin." Koko has a 7-7-J and 6.

By this time, the pot is up to $13.25, which was a lot in those days, and an awful lot in prison. Koko starts freaking out, wondering if Luke has been bluffing the whole time or if he really does hold a king in his hand.

The dealer yells at Koko, "What you gonna do, play like a coconut? You gotta call him."

Koko waffles even though it would only cost him a buck to see Luke's hand. He whines, "I know he's got a pair of kings!"

Most of the prisoners think he's being a wimp and challenge him to call Luke.

Instead, Koko follows the goading of a friend and folds his hand. The inmates bellow in disappointment. Then, in a total breach of poker etiquette, Koko's friend reaches over and flips Luke's card up, showing he had nothing, not even a pair.

Koko's friend laughs, "Nothin'. A handful a nothin'. You stupid mullethead. He beat you with nothin'." Then he looks at Luke and chides him that he is a man full of nothin'.

"Yeah, well," Luke says, with a smirk on his face as he pops the cap off a bottle of soda, "sometimes nothin' can be a real cool hand."

Now is that a great scene or what? It's actually where the movie got its name. Anyway, the reason I bring it up is to ask you to think about Cool Hand Luke's line: "Sometimes nothin' can be a real cool hand." I mean, could that be true? Could there be something in nothing?

Do you remember a while ago when you told me how discouraging it was to be so far behind your friends? They'd moved on with their lives, gotten jobs, married, and some even have kids. You said it would be like starting from scratch when you got out at thirty-one. I get it, and to be honest, I kind of agree with you. In a way, you do have nothing.

But here's a crazy thought for you—just something to think about. Wouldn't it be wild if, instead of being discouraged about your nothing, you actually embraced it? Imagine if you owned it, like really owned it, with your whole heart. Imagine admitting it out loud to yourself, actually saying, "I've got nothin'." Saying it to yourself in the mirror, leaning in, getting real close, saying it slowly. Then a second time. What if you caressed it like Gollum did the ring? What if you shouted it to the prison yard and at the trees and whispered it at night as you fell asleep? Over and over, you just admit, "I've got nothin'."

I know, I know, this may seem over-the-top, but here's my thinking: sometimes admitting a truth and owning it with vigor, strips it of its power. All of a sudden, it becomes less scary, less intimidating; you're not so possessed by it or afraid of it or haunted by it. They're even using this technique with soldiers returning home from war, asking them to retell their traumatic stories over and over, hoping they will lose some of their potency over time.

I don't know, it's just an idea.

But now that we're playing this game, can I take it one step further? Instead of just doing these mental gymnastics, why don't you explore whether there actually is something in the nothing. In other words, as Cool Hand Luke says, maybe nothin' can be a real cool hand.

Here's how I thought of it for you.

Nothin' brought you to your knees. You were one hard dude, maybe just too cool for life, and to be honest, I never thought you'd humble out. Ever. But this did it. The accident. Rod. Valerie. Prison. It looks like you might have found your bottom. And know this: a humble man is a beautiful man. A man who has seen the darkness, a man who has looked in the mirror and not flinched, a man who has taken his due, a man who is broken but doesn't break—that is a man you gotta respect.

Nothin' brought you gratitude. I think you've become thankful for the simple things in life, like fresh fruit, a home-cooked meal, and the freedom to hike the mountains if you want to. Freedom's a gift that only those who've lost it really understand. But you lost it; you know incarceration; you know submission and humiliation and control. I have a feeling you'll never forget those things and will love your freedom like few men do.

Nothin' brought us together, you and me. Not just because you hit bottom and I was there for you. But because I also hit bottom. I didn't realize it, but when the accident happened, I was a shell of a father and spiritually numb. And really it was because of us reconnecting the way we did, with all those talks and letters, that brought both of us out of the ditch together. I mean who gets that with his son? What father and son share not only DNA, but also a survivor bond?

Nothin' brought you sobriety. To see you slowly—over weeks and months—emerge from the fog of opioids was surreal and thrilling. At first, it was the eyes—they were finally clear. Then the shoulders—they relaxed. Then the depression—it needed to run its course. Then the mind—it woke up with a vengeance.

Finally, and most importantly, nothin' brought you to God. It did! I never thought I'd say that about my Lucas. I know that sounds faithless and negative, but you just seemed too removed from God, or just unable to connect—I'm not sure the reason. But what I do believe is that you would have never leaned into God if it hadn't been for your nothin'.

So, son, I hope you'll think about this and find your own something in the nothin'. And you know, if you do, that may turn out to be a pretty cool hand.

Love, Pops

Years after writing this letter to Lucas, I realized that I, too, had my own version of nothing.

Nothing made me grateful. Like only parents of addicts know, I know how bad it could have been. With about one hundred thousand overdoses annually during the years of Lucas's use, I could so easily have only two sons, or even just one. But no. Now, when my sons come over with their wives on Sunday afternoons, and we rat-a-tat pickleball on our court for a couple hours, hang out in the Jacuzzi afterward, and enjoy some barbecue after that—often, out of nowhere, tears will flood my eyes and I'll look away, overcome with the thought of how empty my house could have been, how easily all this could have *not* been, how different my life could look. And embedded in those tears is the re-alization of the cost to another family. Their loss is never far from my mind. And it never fails to confound me. I don't know the ways of God, or the universe, or why things happen as they do. All I can do is accept what's in front of me, good or bad, and be grateful for it.

Nothing helped me come to peace with what I can't control. I can't force my sons to change. I can't change my wife. I couldn't change my dad. I can barely change myself. And I'm so-so at changing Mumford. I've had to rewrite the Serenity Prayer for myself: "God, grant me the serenity to accept that I can't change anyone, the graciousness to help those I can, and the wisdom to know when to keep my big yapper shut." But having said that, I also don't want to become the cynical, disappointed father who jadedly sits in the corner, stewing in his pessimism, pissed off that he can't run the world as it should be run. No, I want to stay engaged and involved, available to my family when they need me, an optimistic man, perhaps even playful (okay, that's a stretch). I want to be my sons' number one fan (well, actually their number two fan after Joyce), encouraging them to be noble, inspiring them to be selfless, reminding them not to make the same mistakes with their children that I made with them. I want to be all in. And I want to do all of it with a serenity and calmness that honors their agency. God, help me be that kind of dad.

Nothing helped me rediscover God. When there was barely a spiritual pulse, when I was haunted by loss and tormented with discouragement, I opened a dusty Bible and read a story about an old friend named David. Turning off my computer and closing my Bible that day, I remember feeling the tiniest flicker of hope that maybe I wasn't lost after all, maybe I'd find my way back to God, maybe there would be another chapter for me. I had no idea what that might look like at the time, but I knew I didn't want to end my faith bitterly, shaking my fist at the heavens and cursing God. Maybe I could recover like David did.

I have one last nothing to share. It's not my nothing and it's not Lucas's. It's the nothing that Rod and Valerie experienced. It's the nothing that still takes my breath away and dogs me every single day. For theirs is the true nothing, the ultimate nothing, an irretrievable, inconsolable, excruciating nothing. And it hovers over every word in this book and every page. Each time I sat in front of my computer to write, even as I was drowning in my own pain, their nothing hung in my mind as a constant presence, driving me on, humbling me, troubling me, and compelling me to put words on the page.

For years, May 25, 2016, the day of the accident, was a date I was unable to process. What happened on that day was so unfair and capricious that it churned, unresolved in my psyche. At one point, I got so desperate to find solace that I even looked for help in a place my Christian self would have never looked: reincarnation. For months I researched that belief system to see if it might bring some resolution to my discontent. I found no solace there.

Finally, I caught a ray of light on February 12, 2021, the second anniversary of Lucas's release from prison. That morning, I journaled for over an hour, trying once again to find a little perspective on what happened that day. This is part of what I wrote.

Two years ago, Lucas was released from the control of the State of California. As I think about it, his penalty was paltry compared to his crime. But he did serve the time given to him, and now, in his early thirties, he's starting his life over again. He's been given a second chance.

I continue to struggle, though, with the inequity of it all: the loss of Rod's life, the way Valerie's life was blown up. I just can't reconcile it, and it always pulls on my gut. The events that day in May feel like a river that has flowed past me and I keep grabbing downstream water, trying to pull it back as if I'm trying to pull back time. There are times I wonder if true justice would have been Lucas also losing his life. Otherwise, it feels like there's an imbalance in the universe, a hiccup in the natural order of things, something that needs to be made right.

But would that make it right? I mean, would taking Lucas's life do it? Does there need to be an eye for an eye? I don't know.

Maybe in this fallen world, an eye does not need to be taken for an eye. Maybe there is room for people to make mistakes, to do terrible things, to hurt people, maybe even on purpose at the time, and yet still have a penalty they can pay that is short of death. Our entire system has created particular punishments that fit certain crimes. They don't equalize the crime. They don't make the victim whole. But they are what we, as flawed humans, can reasonably come up with.

As I think about Lucas's penalty, I realize it was neither fair nor unfair. But it was the penalty that society and the justice system gave him. And he paid it.

Maybe I just need to accept that. This was a tragedy; it was not fair, it never will be fair, and we handled it in the best way we could.

I've often wondered if I will meet Valerie one day. She's frequently on my mind, hovering in the background, as I remember her on the day of sentencing—sad, bewildered, and, most painfully to me, surrendered. She seemed beaten up from the twisting of events that swarmed her life. And if I'm conscious the moments before I die, I will think of her, I will remember her, I will pay homage to her, and bow my head to pray for her. And for Rod.

As I write about our nothings, I must admit, I'm scared. Not at what I've shared, or confessed, or how it made me or Lucas look. I have no doubt some will tar me as the worst father ever. Others will doubt whether I was ever even a Christian, much less one now. And others will prophesy my imminent divorce from Joyce. But at my age, and after all I've been through, I really don't care anymore.

My true fear is that writing about Lucas will put pressure on him and weigh him down. What if he slips up, what if he relapses, what if he doesn't become the man he aspired to be while in prison? I don't want him to feel that weight from me or my writing. Life will be difficult enough for him to handle.

I'm also nervous, though, for me, too. What will I do if he relapses after hanging out all our dirty laundry? Will I feel the fool? Will I curl back into myself and my solitude and venture back deeper and deeper into the Sierra with Mumford? Will I go numb again with God?

Lucas and I have talked about these concerns many times—when he was in prison, when he was freshly out, and for years since. Each time

I've brought it up, he has insisted on the same thing: he wants the story told. Even though it chronicles the lowest moments of his life, he knows the story is bigger than he is. It must be told for others' sake. Others are also staring at their own nothing, and they need to see their own flicker of light; they need to find their something in the nothing. And if this book can be that flicker, even for just one person, then Lucas's nothing, and my nothing, and the nothing which bleeds through this book, may turn into someone else's something.

26

Mom's Spaghetti

I know Lucas requested his mom's spaghetti as his come-home meal, but I cheated. I had fresh salmon belly in the fridge, which I pulled out as soon as he walked into the kitchen at about noon on the day of his release. He could not resist. He dipped the translucent orange flesh into wasabi soy sauce, plopped it on some rice, and thrust it into his mouth. He didn't stand up on the kitchen chair and belt out the "Hallelujah Chorus" from Handel's *Messiah*, but he did roll his eyes and groan and smile like a man who had just spent three years eating cafeteria food. He was home. Now he was really home.

Joyce had picked him up at about eight that morning from CRC. She stood beside her car in one of the parking lots, having been instructed to remain next to it until a van arrived. Lucas was the last inmate to step out of the van, and once he spotted Joyce, he hurried over to her with a smile on his face. As he got close, he picked up his pace and broadened his smile. Their embrace was tight and long, filled with what only a mother and son can feel after three years of incarceration.

She had wanted to pick him up by herself. I'm not sure exactly why, but she'd asked, and I had agreed without much thought. I don't think it was a concern about us talking over each other—we were past that—I just think she wanted to be there for that special moment. She wanted to be there when he walked into free air, away from the cauldron of tight control, frivolous rules, blatant racism, endless lines, incessant talking, brute existence, and lukewarm coffee—into a world of relaxed breathing, spontaneous mobility, quiet bedrooms, and brewed coffee.

Once he crawled into the passenger seat, he was a little jittery, and asked, "Can we get out of here right away?" His pitch was high, and his voice was quivering.

She threw the car into first gear, and they were on the highway in minutes.

A few miles from our house, while still heading north on Highway 14, Lucas asked Joyce to stop by the scene of the accident. She hadn't expected this but agreed to exit at Placerita Canyon Road. As she merged onto the off-ramp, he asked, "Why are you getting off here?"

"Well, this is where it happened. Just down this road."

"Here? It happened here?" he asked, seeming bewildered. "Why would I have exited here that day?"

"Well, we've all wondered that for years," she said. A quarter mile down the road, she pulled the car onto the shoulder and came to a stop. "It happened right over there, where that white bike is propped up against the oak tree. Some of the cyclists in the area put it there to commemorate Rod's death."

Lucas grimaced. He asked if he could have a minute. Joyce tried to give him his privacy but peeked and saw him staring at the white-painted ghost bike. Lucas told me later he had no memory of ever being in that spot and little memory of what happened that day. All those years in prison, he'd tried to arrange the jigsaw pieces of his memory to form a picture of the place where all their lives had changed forever. He studied the area, looking beyond the bike into the oak grove, then up at the hills and the mountains, then back across the road, then back toward the highway. So, this was it. This was the spot.

He bowed his head and prayed.

Once back in the car, he asked Joyce for one more stop before they got home. This time it was Vons grocery store so he could get some personal items.

"This is unbelievable," Lucas gushed, as he viewed the endless selection of deodorants. "I had no idea there were so many kinds." He slowly walked the aisles, in awe of the shelves sagging from their abundance.

When he walked through our front door, he and I also had a long, firm embrace. It was awkward for about ten seconds, just getting used to this man who had so occupied our lives for three years, now standing in our house. But then we settled in. After the salmon belly, friends of ours started to come over to see him. One by one, they, too, got their long hugs and were able to wet his cheeks with their tears.

The following Monday, a friend of ours who owned a construction company picked Lucas up for work. He hasn't missed a day since.

The next weekend, he asked if he could accompany me to the church service at Reality LA, the place he'd heard so much about. And, as I'd suspected, it was just not the same. Having him with me changed everything. I couldn't relax into my old cathartic groove or feel the angst that had always driven me to that place. I couldn't cry out to God for someone who was now standing right next to me, smiling, and singing and ready to get on with his life. Suddenly my lostness and sorrow and confusion felt foreign to me, like an ill-fitting jacket. I haven't been to Hollywood since.

Lucas joined an AA-type group at a local church and completed their program over the next year. He graduated and was baptized at the same time. A year later, he married a beautiful young woman from our old church, Danica, whom we'd known almost her whole life. The wedding was in our backyard with my siblings in attendance, all their kids, and a hundred family friends. On that cool Southern California night, the tears flowed freely, and the dancing was infused with a reckless abandon that only comes from a long story like ours, a gratitude like ours, and an ending like ours. At eleven that evening, the cops showed up to issue me a ticket for violating the sound ordinance. But as they gave me the ticket, one of them pulled me aside and said, "I gotta confess to you, it is so good to see people having a good time after all this COVID mess." After they left, I smiled to myself and thought, *It is so good to see people having a good time after* our *mess.*

In the fall of 2022, Lucas, Danica, and Danica's daughter, Riley, welcomed a boy named Finnley into the world.

Lucas still works the construction job he started three days after his release. He still reads, although not voraciously. And on occasion, he orders the salmon belly at Love Sushi and recalls the eleven-year-old boy who tried it, the twenty-five-year-old lost soul who scarfed it, and the changed thirty-one-year-old man who savored it as his first meal after prison.

Epilogue

I t was a good thing, writing to my son when he was in prison. It helped him, and it bonded the two of us for life. We experienced what few fathers and sons ever will. No matter what happens to us, I wrote what I wrote, and he wrote what he wrote. No one can take that away from us.

But really, I think it helped me most of all. It brought into focus what happened in my family and the role I played in it. I blew it that fall of 2002, and it all cascaded from there. Jess freaked out. Lucas glommed on to Jess. And Chris absorbed that radiation for years. At least now I see when it was that I ignored my instincts and signed on with the wrong team. And now that I know, I'm better for it. And maybe my story will help others. I think it will help my sons, who now have sons and daughters of their own. Maybe it will help other parents to silence the static in their world so they can hear the quiet, still voice inside of them that has guided parents since the beginning.

My sons are okay after all this family drama—they are none the worse for the wear. And now they, too, face the intimidating task of parenting children without exasperating them. They, too, will have their own In-N-Out and Winter Formal, and if they are lucky (or, if their kids are lucky), they will remember the lessons I learned and know when to hold 'em and when to fold 'em, when to play bad cop and when to let nature do what she does best, when to relax their grip and when to tighten it, and above all, when to listen to that godly voice inside themselves.

I'm one of the lucky ones, I know that. All my sons are alive. I know that as only someone who came so close to the edge can know it. They each married good, kind, gracious women, including Chris, who now also enjoys sobriety and a great career. They love me and Joyce and our house and, maybe most of all, our pickleball court. Hanging out with "the fam bam" is their favorite activity in all the world (their words). Who gets that? It's as good now as it was bad back then.

But now that just humbles me. Without my darkness, I would have arrogantly attributed it to "just great parenting." If I hadn't struggled, I would have been smug and haughty and looked down my religious nose at those who didn't discipline their kids or take them to church or go to all their sports games or stimulate them intellectually or love them like I did.

But now I just look up from my Jacuzzi at night and raise my palms to the southern stars, swearing I can feel a cosmic vibration from that vast universe telling me that I am something in this speckled darkness. I often find myself whispering, *thank you, thank you, thank you*. Now when I'm high up in the mountains, in the early dawn, hiking westward, and the sun rises behind me, giving me a glimpse of alpenglow, I pause, leaning on my hiking poles, and whisper, *thank you, thank you, thank you*.

For I have found a place that can't be described or found on any map. It's a place that requires a steep price for entry, a price you cannot volunteer to pay, one that money will not buy. Its price is darkness, extended darkness, darkness you thought would never end. Only a family who has seen this darkness, and seen it for years, can know this place. And when you're there—that place with no name, that place where the boundary lines are good again—you do not speak of it, you do not breathe a word, even to your spouse, even to yourself, lest it vanish, lest it disappear as quietly as it arrived, on cat's paws, in the still of morning.

You also know, now, in your heart, that life will not always be good. And when it turns, when the goodness is swallowed up by that which is not good, whatever that may be, in whatever form that may take, you recall this verse:

When times are good, be happy. When times are bad, remember that God made one as well as the other.

Acknowledgments

My first reader and my biggest fan is my wife, Joyce. When Lucas went to prison, she searched for a book to help her stay sane and make sense of this part of her life. But she couldn't find one. As I started piecing this book together, she strongly encouraged me forward so that other parents would have something to help them make sense of a similarly crazy time in their lives. Well, honey, I think we have such a book. Your five-exclamation-point comments from the beginning helped me see that I had something to say to people who had lost their way with their children, lost their way with their God, and feared they'd lose their way with each other.

Nan Wiener, my main editor, was hugely instrumental in focusing this book, even though I'd been at it for five years. Finding her was a breath of fresh air. Her perspective as a spouse and a parent helped me develop those themes in the book. Although not particularly religious, she asked all the right questions and identified all the right areas for me to focus on when writing about my faith. She was a cheerleader, a believer in my message, a constant comma-corrector, a re-worder, a sounding board on long phone calls, and the singular person I needed in order to complete a book I can feel good about. Thank you, Nan!

Lucia Joyce, a fellow writer I met in an online class, became much more than that. In the class I noticed her insight and reached out to her a year later to have her read some of what I had written. She was so insightful with her observations that I hired her right then, even though she was working as a dancer on a cruise ship in the Mediterranean. She pushed me to add more specifics and flesh out some scenes, and to include more of Joyce in the book. One time, after I'd written a small anecdote about Joyce's reaction in a scene, she wrote, "Yes, yes! I can't get enough of Joyce." (Maybe it was because they both share a name?) So thank you, Lucia.

Kim Thompson was my earliest reader when the book was a mish-mash of ideas and letters and essays and journal entries and emotional outpourings. She read everything I sent her, offered early direction, and identified where my writing was touching a chord. I could not have done this without her. Thank you, Kim.

Liz Cotone, one of my earliest editors, was also a believer, seeing the need for this book in the world. She offered keen insights and suggestions for where to take the story.

To the writing professionals who instructed me well, Karin Gutman, Marion Roach Smith, Allison Langer, Michele Orwin (my very first editor), and Connie Hale (with her beautiful Hawaiian ethos), I thank you.

To my early readers, Stacy Zike, Tom Jones, Gloria Rabil, Cathy Byrd, Nick Sweeney, Evan Dooling, Jeanne Oldfather, Mike Hammer, Tom Hedman, and Paul Dillman, thank you.

Dave Lyznick, thanks for taking those notes at the hearing and for just loving our family.

To Greg Smith, my fellow creative, whether on the court or off. Thanks for being there at Starbucks while I was experiencing what I write about in this book, and for being the best listener I've ever known. You and Betty showed unfailing interest in this story and continually cheered me on.

To the Bublish team, especially Kathy Meis, who "got" the story right away and saw its potential, for guiding me through the labyrinth of publishing a book myself. Thanks for being so responsive and patient and insightful.

To Rod and Valerie. I have tried to honor your lives in this book. I'm sure I fell short, but I attempted to do so with all my heart. I will never forget you and I hope the world doesn't either.

To Jess and Chris, thanks for our epiphanies while sitting in the Jacuzzi, trying to figure out what happened to our family, when it happened, and why it happened. And for continually encouraging me to keep it real, no matter how embarrassing or brutal.

And finally, to Lucas. What we've experienced, I wouldn't wish on any father and son. But it's bonded us like few fathers and sons will ever experience. To be there when you broke down, when you came face-to-face with justice, to hear you respond to David, to listen to you wax on about C.S. Lewis, and then to receive your *Two Men* letter hauntingly contrasting our two lives...I don't know...who gets that? What father is so privileged, so privy to his sons highs and lows? I don't have an answer. I just know that it happened, and we will both never be the same for it. I hope we can make our story a blessing to others.

About the Author

K en Guidroz is a late-in-life writer who has had several careers: pharmaceuticals, ministry, and since 2005, designing retirement plans for companies. In 2010 he coauthored a popular business book, *Beyond the 401(k)*. Two years later he cofounded a training program for financial advisors called *Cash Balance Coach* which has educated thousands.

Personal writing, however, is his passion—and has become a lifesaver. It started when he wrote extensively in his journal to stay sane while his

The Author and Mumford

sons struggled with addiction, then continued when he wrote to Lucas while he was in prison, and culminated with this book about reconnecting with Lucas, fatherhood, marriage, and faith. He hopes to continue his writing journey by developing many of the themes found in this book in a newsletter. And by calling it a *newsletter*, he places the emphasis on "letter."

Join his email list on his website, www.KenGuidroz.com

Ken lives in Santa Clarita, California, with his wife, Joyce, to whom he has been married for over forty years. His three sons and their families all live close by. He loves all things racket-sports and most recently finds himself addicted to pickleball. He hikes the mountain behind his house early every morning with his dog, Mumford, and they also spend weeks every year hiking deep into the Eastern Sierra mountains, camping in his tricked-out van.

Printed in the USA
CPSIA information can be obtained
at www.ICGtesting.com
JSHW020507070823
46061JS00002B/149